CHRIST *the* HEALER

CHRIST *the* HEALER

F. F. BOSWORTH

Foreword by ROBERT V. BOSWORTH

Chosen
a division of Baker Publishing Group
Grand Rapids, Michigan

© 1924, 1948 by F. F. Bosworth
Forewords © 1973, 2000 by R. V. Bosworth
"The Ultimate Triumph" © 2000 by R. V. Bosworth

Published by Chosen Books
A division of Baker Publishing Group
P.O. Box 6287, Grand Rapids, MI 49516-6287
www.chosenbooks.com

New paperback edition published 2008

Printed in the United States of America

Library of Congress Cataloging-in-Publication Data
Bosworth, F. F. (Fred Francis), 1877–1958.
    Christ the healer / F. F. Bosworth ; foreword by Robert V. Bosworth. — Rev.
and expanded ed.
        p. cm.
    ISBN 978-0-8007-9457-6 (pbk.)
    1. Spiritual healing. I. Title.
    BT732.5.B67 2008
    234'.131—dc22   2008021876

Unless otherwise indicated, Scripture is taken from the King James Version of the
Bible.

Scripture marked ASV is taken from the American Standard Version of the Bible.

Contents

Foreword to the 2000 Edition   7
Foreword to the 1973 Edition   10
Author's Preface   13

Sermon
 1 To Those Needing Healing   15
 2 Did Jesus Redeem Us from Our Diseases When He
    Atoned for Our Sins?   24
 3 Is Healing for All?   49
 4 The Lord's Compassion   73
 5 How to Appropriate the Redemptive and Covenant
    Blessing of Bodily Healing   91
 6 Appropriating Faith   116
 7 How to Receive Healing from Christ   123
 8 How to Have Your Prayers Answered   138
 9 The Faith That Takes   143
10 Our Confession   150
11 Fullness of God's Life: The Secret of Victory   160
12 God's Garden   166
13 Why Some Fail to Receive Healing from Christ   175
14 Paul's Thorn   202

Thirty-one Questions   220
Testimonies   226
The Ultimate Triumph   251

F. F. BOSWORTH

Foreword to the 2000 Edition

Christ the Healer, first published by my late father, F. F. Bosworth, in 1924, has been in continual print for 76 years. The book has been the living pioneer classic and textbook on the subject of God's compassion and longing to heal all who are sick. It lives because of the current flood of testimonies from those spiritually feeding directly on my father's ministry through the book. Other vast multitudes are benefiting through the ministry of countless preachers around the world who are proclaiming the same truth that they have learned through these teachings. It seems to be in order to explain the need to revise, expand and publish another edition of such a successful classic.

My father said in his preface, "In this book we have tried to use the vocabulary that common people understand...." In his day, this goal was accomplished, as evidenced by the stream of testimonies that flooded his ministry office from those converted and healed. Dad's passion was to communicate transforming truth, transferable concepts that would surge forward and spread from one believer to another. He longed to see God's Word grow, creating a domino effect and bringing true revival.

Although the truths published in the early editions never changed, language, writing styles and vocabulary have become more direct. The first messages were made up of long sentences with many compound phrases making comprehension difficult. Many of the newer messages in the eighth edition were presented in a more modern and easy-to-understand way. The older messages were left as they were, and to the younger generations, these became more difficult to understand.

In presenting this limited revision, I have sought to enhance truth without changing it. Long sentences have been broken down and the concepts have been checked for clarity. I have been very careful to maintain the integrity of truth as stated in the old text.

At the time the original book was published, my dad was experiencing much ministry pressure, and he felt strongly the necessity to publish printed truth for the masses. Never having developed writing skills, he merely gathered his most important sermons and put them in a logical sequence. His book became a compilation of sermons. The sermons were written in the same style as he preached. Proof-texts and references were kept to a minimum. Many quotations of the Word were from translations and helpful paraphrases unavailable today. He had a habit of using quotation marks to emphasize a truth, not always a quotation. Because of the necessity in ministry to recap previous truths, there is a certain repetition and overlapping in the sermons presented. I have not revised or edited these.

Little has been written concerning the life and ministry of F. F. Bosworth and his brother, Bert, as it relates to *Christ the Healer* and their healing ministry. Dad and B. B.

were dedicated evangelists. To them, the saving of souls was paramount, and every other consideration, including the healing of the body, was secondary. Early in Dad's ministry, he discovered that the healing side of the Gospel had been given to the Church as its greatest evangelizing agency. This discovery continued to guide him through more than fifty years of ministry. This guiding light eventually took him to Africa at the age of 75, where he had his most successful ministry.

Christ the Healer has been expanded to briefly cover Dad's testimony of healing and successful ministry after the age of 75.

In the preface to this book, F. F. Bosworth expressed his earnest prayer that many thousands would learn to make the promises of God's Word work in their lives. With this thought in mind, we present the new revised and expanded edition of *Christ the Healer*.

Bob Bosworth

Foreword to the 1973 Edition

Little did I realize, when I published the first popular paper-back edition of this book, what a surge of new interest would be generated. When the dust of skepticism, kicked up by the mercenary methods of a decade of "faith healers," had finally settled, there was a deep hunger in the hearts of many sincere Christians for a sane and scriptural presentation of irrefutable Bible truth.

Many men of God have been aware that the Reformation has never been completed, that God seems to be systemati-cally working toward a return to New Testament faith and simplicity so as to eternally silence man's excuse of ignorance of God's message. Fundamental Christianity has suffered great damage through the efforts of some theologians to excuse their own spiritual impotence through relegating everything supernatural into an imaginary transition period of dispensational truth, which cannot be scripturally proven. It can only be substantiated through their own interpreta-tion of isolated passages and is perpetrated through blind traditionalism not unlike that which Christ faced. Yet, deep within the hearts of sincere men, there is a longing to rescue the book of Acts from becoming nothing more than a historical record and to put it back in its proper place as a pattern for the modern Church. In this way God can continue to confirm His Word and give proof of the resurrection of His Son in this day of universal unbelief.

When the first simple truths concerning God's attitude toward sickness and human suffering came to my father as a result of intensive study of Scripture, it was like a bright light in a traditional darkness. Not only did God illuminate Scripture, but He confirmed His Word through Dad's personal ministry, healing those beyond the help of medical science. The Word also produced a depth of holiness in their lives. I'm sure my father did not realize that the truth received was fifty years ahead of its time. Only after it had been proven through Dad's life and ministry, could it be used as a major contribution in God's reformation process of returning supernatural power to His Church.

Medical science has made great strides in its effort to alleviate human suffering. Yet the accelerated pace of our modern society continues to take its toll on the bodies of men and women, producing sickness beyond a man's ability to help. The demands for sufficient doctors, hospitals, beds and cures grow with increasing pressure, and many new drugs and medicines are creating new problems. The population explosion has caused problems of poverty, malnutrition and epidemic disease that can only intensify the message that man needs a healer God. How the father nature of God must long for man to return to the security and simple faith of pure fellowship with Him, taking His Word as fact that can be fully trusted!

It is within the context of human need that the greatest message of this book shines forth as a beacon in a faithless world. Basically the Church has only one message: In all things, our Heavenly Father can be trusted to honor His Word. Beyond just the message of divine healing, this book clearly presents the principles of faith in a way whereby every Christian can discover and possess, through the benefits of Calvary, all that Adam lost. It is to hungry, needy men and women everywhere that we present this new edition of *Christ the Healer.*

R. V. Bosworth

Author's Preface

When, in the year 1924, we wrote the messages for the first edition of this book, little did we dream that the truths presented were to bless such vast numbers in so many parts of the world. The results, down through the years, have been a demonstration of the truth of the inspired declaration that God "is able to do exceeding abundantly above all that we ask or think" (Ephesians 3:20).

During the forty-four years that have followed, six more large editions have been printed and read by thousands of ministers and laymen who have written to us telling how they have been enlightened and blessed, soul and body, through reading and rereading these messages.

In this book we have tried to use the vocabulary common people understand. A continual stream of testimonies comes to us from those soundly converted and miraculously healed through their own faith, which came to them while reading and meditating on the truths of the Bible, which we have tried to make plain.

We have proved thousands of times, and are continuing to prove, that by the simple presentation of enough of the written Word of God to the minds and hearts of the incurably afflicted, they can be brought to the same state of certainty and assurance concerning the healing of their body as to the healing of their soul.

We are therefore increasingly thrilled over the privilege of planting the "incorruptible seed," the Word of God, in the hearts of those for whom Jesus died. O what a glorious fact that we have each been "bought with a price" to be the Lord's garden in which His "imperishable seed," the Word, is to be continually "planted," "watered" and "cultivated," so that it can produce present and eternal wonders.

In the "seed" there are possibilities beyond the power of the human mind to conceive, just as in a little seed there is a potential tree a million times bigger than the seed. All of God's wonderful works are potentially in the seed. By keeping God's garden planted, as the farmer does his fields, a child of God can accomplish things a thousand times greater than men of the highest human talents can accomplish, by receiving His promises.

We have found that those who have tuned in the broadcasts of the National Radio Revival, most of whom we have never seen, by reading the healing and other literature we have published, get a much broader understanding than those who hear only an occasional message in our public meetings. Because they can be reread and studied, our messages in printed form produce better results in the souls and bodies of those for whom we pray than in some who attend our meetings and desire to be prayed for before they hear enough of the Word of God to produce faith.

This book is sent out with the earnest prayer that many thousands more may learn to appropriate the many blessings promised in the Bible. "We desire that every one of you . . . [be] followers of them who through faith and patience inherit the promises" (Hebrews 6:11–12).

F. F. Bosworth

1

To Those Needing Healing

Before people can have a *steadfast* faith for the healing of their body, they must be rid of all uncertainty concerning God's will in the matter. Appropriating faith cannot go beyond one's knowledge of the revealed will of God. Before attempting to exercise faith for healing, one needs to know what the Scriptures plainly teach, that it is just as much God's will to heal the body as it is to heal the soul. The sermons in this book point out and explain those portions of Scripture that will forever settle this point for you. It is only by knowing that God promises what you are seeking that all uncertainty can be removed and a steadfast faith is made possible. His promises are each a revelation of what God is eager to do for us. Until we know what God's will is, there is nothing on which to base our faith.

It is important that the mind of those seeking healing be "renewed" so as to be brought into harmony with the mind of God. This is revealed in the Bible and pointed out in the following pages. Faith for the appropriation of God's promised blessings is the result of knowing and acting on God's Word (Romans 10:17). The right mental attitude, or the "renewed mind" (Romans 12:2), makes steadfast faith possible to all.

We are constantly receiving testimonies from those who, though prayed for repeatedly without success, were afterwards wonderfully healed while reading this book. Many also have been happily converted while reading these instructions.

It would surprise the world if they could read the wonderful testimonies that have come to us from all over the country. We have received more than 225,000 letters from our radio listeners and their friends, most of whom we have never seen.

The truths discussed in this book of sermons, together with "the prayer of faith," have brought healing within the grasp of many thousands of sufferers, who would not have recovered without the direct action of the Holy Spirit. To God be all the glory.

While we rejoice in these miracles, we remember that they are only external manifestations of a thousand times greater and more precious miracle that has transpired within the sacred chamber of the inner soul. The inner *cause* is so much more precious than the outward *effect*. External results from prayer are like figures in a bank book that show that you have gold deposited in the bank. The gold is more valuable than the figures.

The Word Is the Seed

Jesus said, "The Word is the seed." It is the seed of the divine life. Until the person seeking healing is *sure* from

God's Word that it is God's will to heal *him*, he is trying to reap a harvest where there is no seed planted. It would be impossible for a farmer to have faith for a harvest before he was *sure* the seed had been planted.

It is not God's will that there shall be a harvest without the planting of the seed—without His will being known and acted on. Jesus said, "*Ye shall know the truth*, and the *truth* shall make you free." *Freedom from sickness comes from knowing the truth.* God does nothing without His Word. "He sent His Word and it healed them" are the words of the Holy Spirit (Psalm 107:20 Fenton's translation). "All His work is done in faithfulness" to His promises.

For each sick person to *know* that it is God's will to heal him, it is necessary for the "seed" to be planted in his mind and heart. It is not *planted* until it is known and received and trusted. No sinner can become a Christian before *he* knows that it is God's will to save *him*. It is the Word of God, planted and watered and steadfastly trusted, which heals both soul and body. The "seed" must *remain* planted and be kept watered before it can produce its harvest.

For one to say, "I believe the Lord is *able* to heal me" before he knows from God's Word that He is *willing* to heal *him*, is like a farmer saying, "I believe God is able to give me a harvest, without any seed being planted and watered." God can't save the soul of a man before the man himself *knows* God's will in the matter. Salvation is by faith—that is, by trusting the *known* will of God. Being *healed* is being *saved* in a *physical* sense.

Praying for healing with the faith-destroying words, "if it be Thy will," is not *planting* the "seed"; it is destroying the seed. "The prayer of faith" that heals the sick is to *follow* (not precede) the planting of the "seed" (the Word). Faith is based on this alone.

It is the *Gospel,* which the Holy Spirit says, "is the power of God unto salvation" in all its phases, both physical and spiritual. *All* the Gospel is for "every creature" and for "all nations." The Gospel does not leave a man in uncertainty praying with an "if it be Thy will"; it tells him what God's will *is.* The Holy Spirit's words, "Himself . . . bare our sicknesses" (Matthew 8:17), are just as truly a part of the Gospel as His words, "Who his own self bare our *sins* in his own body on the tree" (1 Peter 2:24).

Neither the spiritual nor the physical phase of the Gospel is to be applied by prayer alone. Seed is powerless until it is planted. Many, instead of saying, "Pray for me," should first say, "Teach me God's Word, so that I can intelligently cooperate for my recovery." We must know what the benefits of Calvary are before we can appropriate them by faith. David specifies: "Who *forgiveth* all thine iniquities, who *healeth* all thy diseases."

After being sufficiently enlightened, our attitude toward *sickness* should be the same as our attitude toward *sin.* Our purpose to have our *body* healed should be as definite as our purpose to have our *soul* healed. We should not ignore any part of the Gospel. Our Substitute bore both our sins and our sicknesses that we might be delivered from them. Christ's bearing of our sins and sicknesses is surely a valid reason for trusting Him *now* for deliverance from both. When, in prayer, we definitely commit to God the forgiveness of our *sins,* we are to believe, on the authority of His Word, that our prayer is heard. We are to do the same when praying for healing.

We can be sufficiently enlightened by the promises of God by simply believing that our prayer is heard before we have experienced the answer (Mark 11:24). Following this with the observance of Hebrews 10:35–36, we can *always* bring to pass the fulfillment of any divine promise.

It is God's will for every Christian to successfully practice Hebrews 6:11–12.

Between the time we definitely commit to God the healing of our body and the completion of our healing, we can, and should, learn one of the most valuable lessons of our Christian life. That lesson is how to observe Hebrews 10:35–36. Only divine promises can make our faith steadfast. After Jonah had prayed for mercy, he did not cast away his confidence because there was no visible proof that his prayer was answered. No, he held fast his confidence and added to it, in advance, the sacrifice of thanksgiving (Jonah 2:9). In Hebrews 13:15 the Holy Spirit commands us all to do this "continually."

God's promises work their wonders while we see and act on *eternal* realities (on His promises, His faithfulness, etc.), as we refuse to be affected by *temporal* things to the contrary. God always fulfills His promises when He can get the right cooperation. He always accepts us and undertakes for us when we observe Mark 11:24 and Hebrews 10:35–36. "With long life will I satisfy him" is God's promise to be appropriated by all (Psalm 91:16).

Comprehensive Instructions

In Proverbs 4:20–22 we have the most comprehensive instructions as to how to receive healing:

> Attend to my words; incline thine ear unto my sayings. Let them not depart from thine eyes; keep them in the midst of thine heart. For they are life unto those that find them, and health to all their flesh.

The Word of God cannot be health to either soul or body before it is heard, received and attended to. Notice here that the Words of God are life only to those that "find" them. If you want to receive life and healing from God, take time to find the words of Scripture that promise these results.

When God's Word becomes health to all your flesh, your cancer will be gone, your tumor will be gone and your goiter will be gone. We have seen the Word, when received and acted on, produce these results thousands of times. The flesh of thousands today is unhealthy flesh because they have failed to "find" and "attend" to that part of God's Word that produces healing. This is the divine method of receiving the blessings that God has provided for us. Many have failed to receive healing simply because they have not followed this method.

God says that when we do as we are told in the Scripture, His Words are made "health to all our flesh." It matters not what particular kind of unhealthy flesh—whether cancer, goiter, tumor—God says, "health to all their flesh." Whose flesh? Those who "find" and "attend" to the Words of God on the subject. This is exactly the same way that the Word of God becomes health to the soul.

In this comprehensive passage, God tells us exactly how to "attend" to His Words. He says, "Let them not depart from thine eyes; keep them in the midst of thine heart." Instead of having your eyes on your symptoms and being occupied with them, let God's Words not "depart from thine eyes." Look at them continually and, like Abraham, wax strong in faith by looking at the promises of God and at nothing else. As the only way a seed can do its work is by being kept in the ground, so the only way that God's "imperishable seed" can "effectually work in us" is by it being kept "in the midst of our hearts." This does not mean occasionally, but continuously. The reason why many have failed is because they have not done this.

Must Do as Farmers Do

When we attend to God's Words by not letting them depart from before our eyes and by keeping them in the midst of our hearts, the seed is in "good ground." This is the kind of ground in which, Jesus says, "It bringeth forth fruit." Paul says, "It effectually worketh." When the farmer gets his seed into the ground, he does not dig it up every day to see how it is doing, but says, "I am glad that is settled." He believes the seed has begun its work. Why not have this same faith in the "imperishable seed"—Christ's Words, which He says are "spirit and life." Believe that they are already doing their work, without waiting to see. If the farmer, without any definite promise, can have faith in nature, why can't the Christian have faith in the God of nature?

The psalmist said, "Thy Word hath quickened me." Paul tells us that it is the *Word*, which "effectually worketh" in them that believe. Every Word of God is "spirit and life" and will work in us when we receive and "attend" to it. When we receive and obey the Word of God, we can say with Paul, "The power of God worketh in me mightily." Thus the *Word* of God becomes the *power* of God. It is "spirit and life." If a field in which the seed has been sown could talk to us, it would say, "The seed worketh in me mightily."

Three Essential Things

This passage in Proverbs shows us the method of obtaining results from the promises in God's Word:

1. There must be *the attentive ear.* "Incline thine ear unto my sayings."

2. There must be *the steadfast look*. "Let them not depart from thine eyes."
3. There must be *the enshrining heart*. "Keep them in the midst of thine heart."

When your eyes are upon your symptoms and your mind is occupied with them more than with God's Word, you have in the ground the wrong kind of seed for the harvest that you desire. You have in the ground seeds of doubt. You are trying to raise one kind of crop from another kind of seed. It is impossible to sow tares and reap wheat. Your symptoms may point you to death, but God's Word points you to life, and you cannot look in these opposite directions at the same time.

Which Kind of Seed Do You Have?

Which kind of seed do you have in the ground? "Let not God's Word depart from thine eyes; keep it in the midst of thine heart." That is, look steadfastly and continuously and only at the evidence God gives for your faith. God says to all incurables, "every one that looketh shall live." The word "looketh" is in the continuous present tense. It does not mean a mere glance, but "let [His Words] not depart from thine eyes; keep them in the midst of thine heart."

The motives that call for our attention are exceedingly powerful. It is our heavenly Father who speaks. All heaven is behind His Words. The things that are spoken are of quickening and invigorating virtue. They are life to such as find them, and health, not only to the soul, but to the body, not to a particular part of it, but to "all their flesh."

A medicine effectual to the cure of a single member of the body might make the inventor wealthy. Here is a medicine for all the flesh—from your head to your feet. Here is a Physician of infinite ability—". . . who healeth all thy diseases."

The Evidence of Things Not Seen

After you have planted your seed, you believe it is growing before you see it grow. This is faith that is "the evidence of things not seen." In Christ we have perfect evidence for faith. Any man or woman can get rid of his or her doubts by looking steadfastly and only at the evidence that God has given for our faith. Seeing only what God says will produce and increase faith. This will make it easier to believe than to doubt. The evidences for faith are so much stronger than those for doubting. Don't doubt your *faith*; doubt your *doubts,* for they are unreliable.

Oh, what a means of blessing is the look of faith to Christ! There is life, light, liberty, love, joy, guidance, wisdom, understanding, perfect health. There is everything in a steadfast look at the Crucified One. No one ever looks in vain to the Great Physician.

Everyone that looked at the brazen serpent, the type of Christ, lived. "And their faces were not ashamed," says the psalmist. They were all, humanly speaking, incurable, but they were both forgiven and healed by looking. He who trusts Christ has no need to be ashamed of his confidence. Time and eternity will both justify his reliance on God.

This book will show those needing healing just what part of the Word of God they are to receive and "attend" to. Some have been miraculously healed while reading the next sermon in this book.

2

Did Jesus Redeem Us
from Our Diseases When
He Atoned for Our Sins?

Note: If you, Reader, have been taught to regard sickness as a "thorn in the flesh," which must remain, we would urge you to read sermon 14 on Paul's thorn before you read any other sermon in this book. Otherwise you will likely miss the force of the scriptural arguments presented in other parts of the book.

Before answering the above question from the Word of God, I invite your attention to a few facts taught in the Scriptures, which bear on this subject.

The Scriptures declare, in Romans 5:12, that "by one man sin entered into the world, and *death by sin.*" Here it is plainly stated that death entered the world by sin. Therefore, it is clear that disease, which is incipient death, entered into the world *by sin*. Since disease entered by sin, its true remedy *must* be found in the redemption of Christ. It is the devil who oppresses (Acts 10:38), so when nature fails, what power can remove disease but the power of the Son of God? As soon as disease has advanced beyond the power of nature to restore, it will result in death in every case unless removed by the power of God. All honest physicians will admit this, for they claim only the power to assist nature, not to heal. In this event, anything that would hinder the power of God thus supplementing nature would make recovery impossible. Accordingly, James says, "Confess your faults one to another . . . *that* ye may be healed," meaning that otherwise ye cannot be healed.

When disease has advanced beyond the power of nature, neither nature, nor the physician, nor even prayer can save the sufferer until he confesses his sins and unless God, for some sovereign purpose of His own, removes the disease. Since disease is a part of the curse, its true remedy must be the cross. Who can remove the curse but God, and how can God *justly* do it except by substitution? The Bible teaches, as one writer puts it, that disease is the physical penalty of iniquity. Since Christ has borne in His body all our physical liabilities on account of sin, our bodies are therefore released judicially from disease. Through Christ's redemption we may all have, as a part of the "earnest of our inheritance," the "life also of Jesus . . . made manifest in our mortal flesh." This supplements nature until our work is finished. In the same way that we may receive the "firstfruits" of our spiritual salvation, we can receive the "firstfruits" of our physical salvation.

Now, to the question: Did Jesus redeem us from our diseases when He atoned for our sins? If, as some teach, healing is not in the Atonement, why were types of the Atonement given in connection with bodily healing throughout the Old

Testament? In the twelfth chapter of Exodus, why were the Israelites required to eat the flesh of the passover lamb for physical strength, unless we, too, can receive physical life, or strength, from Christ? Paul says Christ is "our Passover, sacrificed for us." Seven hundred and sixty-five years after the institution of the passover, we read in 2 Chronicles 30:20 that "the LORD hearkened to Hezekiah, and healed the people" when they kept the Passover. Paul, in 1 Corinthians 11:29–30, speaks of the failure of the Corinthians to rightly "estimate the body" (Weymouth's translation) of "Christ our Passover" as the reason why many among them were "weak and sickly. . . ."

The Lord's Supper is more than an ordinance, because we may partake of Christ while we are partaking of the emblems of His death and the resulting benefits. In Christ there is both bodily and spiritual life. Surely there is no better time for availing ourselves of the privilege of having the "life also of Jesus . . . made manifest in our mortal flesh" (2 Corinthians 4:11).

Healing Taught in Old Testament Types

Again, in Leviticus 14:18 we read of the priest making atonement for the cleansing of the leper. Why an atonement for the leper's healing if healing for us is not in the Atonement of Christ? The types in Leviticus, the fourteenth and fifteenth chapters, show us that it was invariably through atonement that sickness was healed. We need go no further. This is a complete answer to the question we are discussing. All of these typical atonements point to, and prefigure, Calvary.

Again, Jesus tells us, in Luke 4:19, that He was anointed "to preach the acceptable year of the Lord," referring to the Old Testament year of jubilee. This shows us that the year of jubilee is strikingly typical of Gospel blessings. Here He applies the year of jubilee to the Gospel era.

Leviticus 25:9 shows us that no blessing of the year of jubilee was to be announced by the sounding of the trumpet until the Day of Atonement. On this day a bullock was slain as a sin offering, and the mercy seat sprinkled with blood. No mercy was offered until the blood of the Atonement sprinkled the mercy seat, because it would be a judgment seat if not sprinkled with blood. This teaches us that no mercy or blessing of the Gospel is offered to us irrespective of Christ's Atonement.

Recovery of All Lost in the Fall

Through the Fall we lost everything. Jesus recovered all through His Atonement. It was on the Day of Atonement that God said, "Ye shall return every man to his possession." The order in the year of jubilee is, *first* the Atonement, *then* the sounding of the trumpet of the jubilee, with the glad tidings "ye shall return every man to his possession." The order is the same; *first*, Calvary, *then* the Gospel trumpet that He "bare our sins" and "bare our sicknesses," etc., to be sounded "to every creature." This shows us that we may return "every man to his possession."

God's seven redemptive names, one of which is Jehovah Rapha, "I am the LORD that healeth thee," shows us what lost possessions "every man" may return to during our dispensation. The two outstanding possessions to be restored during the Gospel era are health for soul and body. Forgiveness and healing were offered universally wherever Christ preached "the acceptable year of the Lord." The "inner" and "outer" man might then be made whole and ready for the service of

God. All were "thoroughly furnished unto every good work," so they could finish their course.

Some of the Fundamentalists who attack the Christian Scientists for believing we can be saved irrespective of Calvary, make exactly the same blunder when they say they believe in healing but that it is offered irrespective of Calvary. It is to me a mystery how anyone can say that the blood of Christ was just as effective flowing in His veins, as it was after it was shed. Every Old Testament sacrifice had to die and shed blood before the blood was effective. The Bible says, "without the shedding of blood there is no remission of sins." Adopt a bloodless religion and you have but a religion of ideas, and nothing but a human thrill. "Joy unspeakable and full of glory" can never be known except by those who have been saved through the shed blood of Christ. It is just as great a mystery to me how these self-styled Fundamentalists can say that healing is bestowed without reference to Christ's death. The salvation of any part of man without sacrifice is unknown in Scripture.

If bodily healing is offered and is to be preached irrespective of Calvary, why was it that no blessing of the year of jubilee was to be announced by the sounding of the trumpet until the Day of Atonement? Paul tells us that it is "in Him" that all the promises of God are yea and amen. This is another way of saying that all the promises of God, including His promise to heal, owe their existence and power exclusively to the redeeming work of Christ.

Healing Not Deferred until the Millennium

Some ministers are trying to relegate bodily healing to the Millennial Day, but Jesus said *"this day* [not the Millennial Day] is this scripture fulfilled in your ears."

28

It was in the Church (not the millennium) that God set (established) "teachers, miracles, gifts of healing," etc. None in *the Church* will need healing during the millennium, because they will receive glorified bodies before the millennium. They will be caught up to meet the Lord in the air, "when this mortal puts on immortality." If we are going to relegate healing to the millennium, we shall have to do so with the "teachers," etc., that God set in the Church, with the "gifts of healing." To say that healing is only for the millennium is synonymous with saying that we are now in the millennium, because God is healing many thousands in this day.

God's all-inclusive promise is to pour His Spirit upon all flesh during the "acceptable year of the Lord," which is the dispensation of the Holy Spirit. He comes as Christ's executive, to execute for us all the blessings of redemption. He brings to us "the earnest" or "firstfruits" of our spiritual and physical inheritance, until the last enemy, which is death, is destroyed, thus admitting us to our full inheritance.

Faith Comes by Hearing

The reason why many of the sick in our day have not returned to their physical possessions is that they have not heard the trumpet sound concerning healing. "Faith cometh by hearing," and they have not heard because many ministers had their Gospel trumpet put out of order while in the theological seminary. They remind me of a man whom I knew who played a trombone in a brass band. At the beginning of a rehearsal the boys put a small spike into the mouthpiece of his horn. When he blew, his breath went against the head of the spike, making it impossible for him to produce much sound out of the horn. However, he went through the whole rehearsal without discovering what was wrong. Some preachers, like this man, think they are blowing their Gospel trumpet all right. They have not discovered that there is not half as much coming out of it as there ought to be. They are not, like Paul, declaring "the whole counsel of God."

As in Leviticus the types show that healing was invariably through atonement, so Matthew 8:16–17 definitely states that Christ healed all diseases on the ground of the Atonement. The Atonement was His reason for making no exceptions while healing the sick. "He . . . healed all that were sick: that it might be fulfilled which was spoken by Esaias the prophet, saying, Himself took our infirmities, and bare our sicknesses." Since it is our sicknesses He bore, His Atonement embracing us all, it would require the healing of all to fulfill this prophecy. Jesus is still healing all who come to Him with living faith, "that it might be fulfilled. . . ."

Since, in the darker age of the types, they all had the privilege of being healed, surely in this "better" dispensation, with its "better" covenant and "better" promises, God has not withdrawn this Old Testament mercy. If so, we are robbed just that much by the coming and Atonement of Christ.

In Numbers 16:46–50, after 14,700 had died of the plague, Aaron, as priest, in his mediatorial office, stood for the people between the dead and the living and made an atonement for the removal of the plague, the healing of the body. So Christ, our Mediator, by His Atonement, redeemed us from the "plague" of sin and sickness.

The Type of the Brazen Serpent

Again, in Numbers 21:9, we read of the Israelites all being healed by looking at the brazen serpent, which was lifted up as a type of the Atonement. If healing was not to be in the Atonement, why were these dying Israelites required to look at the *type* of the Atonement for bodily healing? Since both healing and forgiveness came through the *type* of the Atonement, why not to us through Christ, the Antitype? As their curse was removed by the lifting up of the brazen serpent, so Paul tells us that ours is removed by the lifting up of Christ (Galatians 3:13).

Again, in Job 33:24–25, we read: "... I have found a ransom [atonement]. His flesh shall be fresher than a child's: he shall return to the days of his youth." Here, we see Job's flesh was healed through an atonement. Why not ours?

Again, David opens the 103rd Psalm by calling upon his soul to bless the Lord and to "forget not all his benefits." Then he specifies, "Who forgiveth all thine iniquities: who healeth all thy diseases." How does God forgive sin? Of course, through the Atonement of Christ. He heals disease in the same way, because the Atonement of Jesus Christ is the only ground for any benefit to fallen man. How can God save any part of man except through the Atonement?

In 1 Corinthians 10:11, Paul tells us "All these things happened unto them for ensamples [as types]; and they are written for our admonition, upon whom the ends of the world [ages] are come." In Galatians 3:7, 16, 29, the Holy Spirit shows us clearly that these things are for Gentiles as well as for Israel. "Know ye therefore that they which are of faith, the same are the children of Abraham. . . . Now to Abraham and his seed were the promises made. . . . And if ye [Gentiles] be Christ's, then are ye Abraham's seed, and heirs according to the promise." "Therefore ye are no more strangers and foreigners, but fellow-citizens with the saints, and of the household of God."

The Reverend Daniel Bryant, in his book *Christ among Our Sick*, says, "The Church then learned what the Church needs, it seems, to learn again; namely, that there is no difference to the compassionate Christ between a sick Gentile and a sick Israelite."

The Seven Redemptive Names of Jehovah

To me, another unanswerable argument that healing is in the Atonement is to be found in the seven redemptive names of Jehovah. On pages 6 and 7 of the Scofield Bible, Mr. Scofield, in his footnote on the redemptive names, says that the name "Jehovah is distinctly the *redemption* name of Deity," and means "the self-existent One who reveals Himself." These seven redemptive names, he says, point to "a continuous and increasing self-revelation." He then says, "In His redemptive relation to man, Jehovah has seven compound names which reveal Him as meeting every need of man from his lost state to the end."

Since it is His *redemptive* relation to us that these names reveal, they *must* each point to Calvary where we were redeemed. The blessing that each name reveals must be provided by the Atonement. This the Scriptures clearly teach.

The following are the seven redemptive names:

JEHOVAH-SHAMMAH is translated "The LORD is there," or present, revealing to us the *redemptive* privilege of enjoying His presence. He says, "Lo, I am with you alway." That this blessing is provided by the Atonement is proven by the fact that we are "made nigh by the *blood* of Christ."

32

JEHOVAH-SHALOM is translated "The LORD our Peace" and reveals to us the *redemptive* privilege of having His peace. Accordingly Jesus says, "My peace I give unto you." This blessing is in the Atonement because "the chastisement of our peace was upon him" when He "made peace through the blood of his cross."

JEHOVAH-RA-AH is translated "The LORD is my Shepherd." He became our shepherd by giving "his life for the sheep," therefore this privilege is a *redemptive* privilege, purchased by the Atonement.

JEHOVAH-JIREH means "The LORD will provide" an offering, and Christ was the offering provided for our complete redemption.

JEHOVAH-NISSI means "The LORD is our Banner," or "Victor," or "Captain." It was when, *by the cross*, Christ triumphed over principalities and powers that He provided for us, through the Atonement, the *redemptive* privilege of saying, "thanks be to God which giveth us the *victory* through our Lord Jesus Christ."

JEHOVAH-TSIDKENU is translated "The LORD our Righteousness." He becomes our righteousness by bearing our sins on the Cross. Therefore, our *redemptive* privilege of receiving "the gift of righteousness" is an atonement blessing.

JEHOVAH-RAPHA is translated "I am the LORD thy Physician," or "I am the LORD that healeth thee." This name is given to reveal to us our *redemptive* privilege of being healed. This privilege is purchased by the Atonement. The redemptive chapter of Isaiah declares, "Surely he hath borne our sicknesses and carried our pains." For the sake of argument, I have reserved this name for the last. The fact is that the very first covenant God gave after the passage of the Red Sea, which was so distinctively typical of our redemption, was the covenant of healing. It was at this time that God revealed Himself as our Physician, by the first *redemptive* and covenant name, Jehovah-Rapha, "I am the LORD that healeth thee." This is not only a promise, it is "a statute and an ordinance." And so, corresponding to this ancient ordinance, we have, in the command of James 5:14, a positive ordinance of healing in Christ's name. This is as sacred and binding on every church today as the ordinances of the Lord's Supper and Christian baptism. Jehovah-Rapha is one of His redemptive names, sealing the covenant of healing. Christ, during His exaltation, could no more abandon His office as Healer than could He abandon the offices of His other six redemptive names. Have any of the blessings that His redemptive names reveal been withdrawn from this "better" dispensation?

Having considered some of the types that teach healing, let us now consider the antitype, the Atonement itself. It is described in the great redemptive chapter, the 53rd chapter of Isaiah. This is the greatest chapter of the greatest of the prophets in which is fully stated the doctrine of atonement. Since the types of the Old Testament taught healing, it is certainly unwarranted and illogical to place the antitype on lower ground.

He Carried Our Pains

Before quoting from this chapter, may I state that the Hebrew words *choli* and *makob* have been incorrectly translated "griefs" and "sorrows." All who have taken the time to examine the original text have found what is acknowledged everywhere. These two words mean, respectively, "sicknesses" and "pains," everywhere else throughout the Old Testament. This word *choli* is interpreted "disease" and "sickness" in Deuteronomy 7:15; 28:61; 1 Kings 17:17; 2 Kings 1:2; 8:8; 2 Chronicles 16:12; 21:15; and other texts. The word *makob* is rendered "pain" in Job 14:22; 33:19; etc. Therefore the prophet is saying, in this fourth verse, "Surely he hath borne our sicknesses, and carried our pains." The reader is referred to any standard commentary for additional testimony on this point; but there is no better commentary than Matthew 8:16–17.

Isaiah 53:4 cannot refer to disease of the soul, and neither of the words translated "sickness" and "pain" have any reference to spiritual matters but to bodily sickness alone. This is proven by Matthew 8:16–17: ". . . and he cast out the spirits with his word, and healed all that were sick: that it might be fulfilled which was spoken by Esaias the prophet, saying, Himself took our infirmities, and bare our sicknesses." This is an inspired commentary on this fourth verse of Isaiah 53. It plainly declares that the prophet refers to bodily ailments. Therefore, the word *sickness, choli*, must be read literally in Isaiah. The same Holy Spirit who inspired this verse quotes it in Matthew as the explanation of the universal application by Christ of His power to heal the body. To take any other view is equal to accusing the Holy Spirit of making a mistake in quoting His own prediction.

I will here quote the learned translator, Dr. Young, in his version of the Bible:

> 3 He is despised, and left of men,
> A man of pains [Heb., *makob*], and acquainted
> with sickness [*choli*],
> And as one hiding the face from us,
> He is despised and we esteemed him not.

4 Surely our sicknesses [*choli*] he hath borne,
And our pains [*makob*] he hath carried them,
And we—we have esteemed him plagued,
Smitten of God and afflicted.

5 And he is pierced for our transgressions,
Bruised for our iniquities,
The chastisement of our peace is on him,
And by his bruise there is healing to us.

6 All of us like sheep have wandered,
Each to his own way we have turned,
And Jehovah hath caused to meet on him
The punishment of us all.

10 And Jehovah hath delighted to bruise him;
He hath made him sick [*choli*]; If his soul doth
make an offering for guilt,
He seeth seed—he prolongeth days.

12 ... With transgressors he was numbered,
And he the sin of many hath borne,
And for transgressors he intercedeth.

Dr. Isaac Leeser, the able translator of the Hebrew English Bible, renders these verses as follows:

3 He was despised and shunned of men:
A man of pains and acquainted with disease.

4 But only our diseases did he bear himself,
And our pains he carried.

5 And through his bruises was healing granted to us.

10 But the Lord was pleased to crush him through disease.

Rotherham's translation of the tenth verse is "He hath laid on Him sickness."

In the fourth verse, the word *borne* (*nasa*) means "to lift up, to bear away, to convey or to remove to a distance." It is a Levitical word and is applied to the scapegoat that bore

36

away the sins of the people. "The goat shall bear [*nasa*] upon him all their iniquities *unto* a land not inhabited: and he shall let go the goat in the wilderness" (Leviticus 16:22). So Jesus bore my sins and sicknesses away "without the camp" to the cross. Sin and sickness have passed from me to Calvary—salvation and health have passed from Calvary to me.

Again, in this fourth verse of the redemption chapter, the Hebrew verbs for "borne" and "carried" (*nasa and sabal*) are both the same as are used in the eleventh and twelfth verses for the *substitutionary* bearing of sin, "He shall bear [carry] their iniquities.... And He bare the sin of many." Both words signify a heavy burden, and denote actual substitution, and a complete removal of the thing borne. When Jesus bore our sins, our sicknesses, and our pains, He bore them away, or removed them. Both these words mean "substitution," one bearing another's load.

On this point, permit me to quote from "Jesus Our Healer," a splendid tract written by the Rev. W. C. Stevens. He says:

> This prophecy presents healing as an integral part of the vicarious Atonement.... Now, whatever be the sense of these two Hebrew verbs (*nasa* and *sabal*), the same sense must be applied in both cases, namely, of sin-bearing and sickness-bearing. To pervert the sense in one case would give liberty to pervert it in the other. And that the sense of the verbs as relating to sin, not only here in this prophecy, but everywhere else in the Old Testament, is strictly vicarious and expiatory, no evangelical student disputes. This prophecy, therefore, gives the same substitutionary and expiatory character to Christ's connection with sickness that is everywhere given to His assumption of our sins.

An Inspired Translation

We are accordingly shut up by the Spirit to the redemptive sense of Christ's bearing of sickness. Freely but faithfully does Matthew 8:17 translate Isaiah 53:4, "Himself took our infirmities, and bare our sicknesses." The help that Jesus rendered in all kinds of bodily sickness is taken in Matthew to be a fulfillment of what in Isaiah is prophesied of the Servant of Jehovah. The Hebrew verbs of the text, when used of sin, speak of a heavy burden, and the bearing away of the guilt of one's sin; that is, to bear sin of another in order to atone for it. But here, where not sins but our sicknesses and our pains are the object, the mediatorial sense remains the same. It is not meant that the Servant of Jehovah merely entered into fellowship of our sufferings, but that He took on Himself the sufferings that we had to bear and deserved to bear; and therefore He not only bore them away, but also in His own Person endured them in order to discharge us from them. Now, when one takes sufferings on oneself that another had to bear, and does this not merely in fellowship with him but in his stead, we call it substitution. Here, then, the best results of rigid exegesis show that the bearing and removal of human disease is an integral part of redeeming work, a provision of the Atonement, a part of the doctrine of Christ crucified; that Jesus is the Savior of the body as well as of the spirit, and that:

> He comes to make His blessings flow
> Far as the curse is found.

Bodily healing by direct divine agency becomes a boon for every believer in any period of Gospel history. It settles the question of a preacher's duty to preach it.

An Objection Answered

A Canadian writer objects that Matthew 8:17 cannot refer to the Atonement because, since Christ had not yet been crucified, this would be "making Christ live an atoning life." This, to me, is no argument at all, since Christ was "the Lamb of God slain from the foundation of the world." He not only healed disease before Calvary, but He also forgave sin, and yet both of these mercies were bestowed on the ground of the Atonement in the future.

A prominent New York clergyman raises practically the same objection. He argues that the fact that Christ, in Matthew, is fulfilling Isaiah's prophecy by healing the sick, proves that "Jesus bore our sickness not on the Cross, but when He was alive in the city of Capernaum." In answering this, I have only to ask, did Jesus bear our *iniquities* in Capernaum or on the Cross? His forgiving of sins as well as His healing of the sick were both done with respect to His coming Atonement, because "without the shedding of blood there is no remission."

The prophecy states that "He hath borne *our* sicknesses." This includes all others, as well as those at Capernaum. In verses 4 and 5 of this redemption chapter, we see Him dying for

"*OUR* sicknesses,"

"*OUR* pains,"

"*OUR* transgressions,"

"*OUR* iniquities,"

"*OUR* peace" and

"*OUR healing*," for "by his stripes we are healed."

We would have to misquote to exclude ourselves from any of these blessings.

The only "surely" in the redemption chapter prefaces His provision for our healing. There could be no stronger statement of our complete redemption from pain and sickness by His atoning death. If Christ, as some think, is unwilling to heal as universally during His exaltation as He did during His humiliation, then He would have to break His promise in John 14:12–13. He would not be "Jesus Christ, the same yesterday, today and forever."

The fact of healing in the Atonement *necessitates* the continuation of His healing ministry during His exaltation. His redeeming work embraces all who live on earth while He is with the Father. Accordingly, He gives the above promise to do the same, and greater works, in answer to our prayers from God's right hand. As long as the Church remained under the control of the Spirit, the same works continued. History reveals, as Dr. A. J. Gordon puts it, "that whenever we find a revival of primitive faith and Apostolic simplicity, there we find the Evangelical miracles which surely characterize the Apostolic age."

The apostle Paul tells us, "He was made sin for us Who knew no sin" (of His own). Likewise, "He hath made Him sick" (for us) Who knew no sickness (of His own). Peter writes, "Who his own self bare our sins in his own body on the tree." Isaiah declares, "Surely our sicknesses he hath borne, and our pains—he hath carried them." Leeser translates, "Only *our* sickness did He bear," having none of His own.

Again, in the sixth verse of Dr. Young's translation cited above, we read, "And Jehovah hath caused to meet on him the punishment of us all." One writer inquires, on this point, "What are the punishments of sin?" He then says, in substance, all will admit that sin is punished by soul-condemnation, remorse, mental anxiety and frequently by sickness . . . and believe these are remitted because of vicarious Atonement.

By what rule of Scripture or reason is the last-mentioned punishment severed from the rest? Mark the prophet's words, "Jehovah hath caused to meet on him the *punishment* of us all." Since sickness is a part of that punishment, it is demonstrated by the immutable Word of God that sickness is included in the Atonement. He then asks, "Is it true that God will give deliverance from every penalty and consequence of sin *except one*, and that this one (sickness) must inevitably remain to the bitter end? Away with such a thought! Isaiah affirms that the *entire* punishment of us all was caused to meet on Him. . . . He testified 'It is finished.' There was nothing incomplete about the work of our mighty Jesus." I might add to this that, were it otherwise, the prophet should have said, "Jehovah hath caused to meet on him only a *part* of the punishment of us all."

The Cross Is a Perfect Remedy for the Whole Man

Jesus went to the cross, spirit, soul and body, to redeem man, spirit, soul and body. Therefore, the cross is the center of the plan of salvation for man, spirit, soul and body.

Every form of sickness and disease known to man was included, and many of them even mentioned particularly, in the "curse of the law," (Deuteronomy 28:15–62, and other Scriptures). In Galatians 3:13, we have the positive statement that "Christ hath redeemed us from the curse of the law, being made a curse for us: for it is written, Cursed is every one that hangeth on a tree." What plainer declaration could we have than that Christ, who was born under the law to redeem us, bore its curse and therefore did redeem us from all sickness and disease. Here it is stated that it was on the cross that Jesus redeemed us from the law's curse. In other words, He redeemed us from the following diseases, specified in Deuteronomy:

"consumption" (tuberculosis), "fever," "inflammation," "the botch of Egypt," "emerods," "scab," "itch," "madness" (insanity), "blindness," "plagues," "all the diseases of Egypt," "also every sickness, and every plague, which is not written in the book of this law." This would include cancer, influenza, mumps, measles and every other modern disease. If Christ redeemed us from the curse of the law, and sickness is included in the curse, surely He redeemed us from sickness.

Redemption Synonymous with Calvary

Redemption is synonymous with Calvary. Therefore, we are redeemed from the entire curse, body, soul and spirit, solely through Christ's Atonement. Since disease is a part of the curse, how could God *justly* remove this part of the curse by healing the sick without first redeeming us from it? Again, since "Christ redeemed us from the curse of the law," how can God justify us and at the same time require us to remain under the law's curse? The apostle Paul says, "Ye are not under the law, but under grace" (Romans 6:14). In short, why should anyone remain under the law's curse who is not under the law? To do so would be the same as putting a man in prison for life after he had been proven innocent and the court had dropped the charge of murder.

Paul argues, in Romans, the third chapter, that "God set forth [Christ] to be a propitiation. . . . that he might be just, and the justifier of him which believeth in Jesus." In other words, were it not for the Atonement, God would be *unjust* in justifying the sinner. Likewise He would be unjust in healing the sick without first redeeming them from the sickness. The fact that God ever healed anyone is to me the best proof that healing was provided by the Atonement. If healing was not provided for all in redemption, how did all in the multitude obtain from Christ the healing that God did not provide? "He healed them *all*."

An Important Question

If the body were not included in redemption, how can there be a resurrection? How can "corruption put on incorruption," or "mortal put on immortality"? If we have not been redeemed from sickness, would we not be subject to disease in heaven, if it were possible to be resurrected irrespective of redemption? Someone has well remarked, "Man's future destiny being both spiritual and bodily, his redemption *must* be both spiritual and bodily."

Why should not the "last Adam" take away all that the "first Adam" brought upon us?

Now, let us consider a few Gospel parallels.

The Inner Man	The Outer Man
Adam, by his fall, brought sin into our souls.	Adam, by his fall, brought disease into our bodies.
Sin is therefore the work of the devil.	Disease is therefore the work of the devil. Jesus "went about doing good, and healing all that were oppressed *of the devil*."
Jesus was "manifested to destroy the works of the devil" in the soul.	Jesus was "manifested to destroy the works of the devil" in the body.
The redemptive name "JEHOVAH-TSIDKENU" reveals God's redemptive provision for our souls.	The redemptive name "JEHOVAH-RAPHA" reveals God's redemptive provision for our bodies.
On Calvary Jesus "*bare our sins*."	On Calvary Jesus "*bare our sicknesses*."
He was made "sin for us" (2 Cor. 5:21) when He "bare our sins" (1 Peter 2:24).	He was "made a curse for us" (Gal. 3:13) when He "bare our sicknesses" (Matt. 8:17).
"Who his own self bare our sins in his body on the tree."	"By whose stripes ye were healed."
"Who forgiveth all thine iniquities."	"Who healeth all thy diseases."

The Inner Man	The Outer Man
"For ye are bought with a price: therefore glorify God in your . . . spirit" (1 Cor. 6:20).	"For ye are bought with a price: therefore glorify God in your body . . ." (1 Cor. 6:20).
The spirit is bought with a price.	The body is bought with a price.
Is remaining in sin the way to glorify God in your spirit?	Is remaining sick the way to glorify God in your body?
Since He "bare *our* sins," how many *must* it be God's will to save, when they come to Him? "Whosoever believeth."	Since He "bare *our* sicknesses," how many *must* it be God's will to heal, when they come to Him? "He healed them all."
"As God made Him to be sin for us who knew no sin."—Rev. A. J. Gordon.	"So God made Him to be sick for us who knew no sickness."—Rev. A. J. Gordon.
"Since our Substitute bore our sins, did He not do so that we might not bare them?"—Rev. A. J. Gordon.	"Since our Substitute bore our sicknesses, did He not do so that we might not bare them?"—Rev. A. J. Gordon.
"Christ bore our sins that we might be delivered from them. Not SYMPATHY—a suffering *with*, but SUBSTITUTION—a suffering *for*."—Rev. A. J. Gordon.	"Christ bore our sicknesses that we might be delivered from them. Not SYMPATHY—a suffering *with*, but SUBSTITUTION—a suffering *for*."—Rev. A. J. Gordon.
"If the fact that Jesus 'bore our sins in His own body on the tree' be a valid reason why we should all trust Him now for the forgiveness of our sins . . .	why is not the fact that He 'bore our sicknesses' an equally valid reason why we should all trust Him now to heal our bodies?" (Writer unknown).
Faith for salvation "cometh by hearing" the Gospel—He "bare our sins."	Faith for healing "cometh by hearing"— He "bare our sicknesses."
Therefore, "Preach the Gospel (that He bore our sins) to every creature."	And "the Gospel (that He bore our sicknesses) to every creature."
Christ's promise for the soul ("shall be saved") is in the Great Commission (Mark 16:16).	Christ's promise for the body ("shall recover") is in the Great Commission (Mark 16:18).
In connection with the ordinance of baptism, the Bible teaches that he that believeth and is baptized shall be saved (Mark 16:16).	In connection with the ordinance of anointing with oil, the Bible teaches that he that believeth and is anointed shall be healed (James 5:14).
We are commanded to baptize in Christ's name.	We are commanded to anoint "in the name of the Lord" (James 5:14).
In the Lord's Supper the wine is taken "in remembrance" of His death for our souls (1 Cor. 11:25).	In the Lord's Supper the bread is eaten "in remembrance" of His death for our bodies (1 Cor. 11:23–24).
The sinner is to repent before believing the Gospel "unto righteousness."	James 5:16 says, "Confess your faults . . . that ye may be healed."

The Inner Man	The Outer Man
Water baptism stands for total surrender and obedience.	Anointing with oil is the symbol and sign of consecration.
The sinner must accept God's promise as true before he can feel the joy of salvation.	The sick must accept God's promise as true before he can feel well.
"As many as received him . . . were born . . . of God" (John 1:12–13).	"As many as touched him were made whole" (Mark 6:56).

Healed through Faith

I will now cite one out of many hundreds of cases of sickness and affliction that have been healed while the sufferers listened to the preaching on the subject of healing in the Atonement. Their healing came through their own faith before having an opportunity of being anointed.

When but a child of eight years, Mrs. Clara Rupert of Lima, Ohio, had such a severe case of whooping cough that she ruptured the muscles of one eye. This left it entirely blind and so dead during all the years that followed that she could rub her finger on the bare eyeball without pain. She said that on windy days, when particles would blow into the eye, it caused her no suffering.

She was listening to a sermon on the Atonement during our revival in Lima, Ohio. She said in her heart: *If that is true, and it is because the Bible says so, then I am just as sure of receiving sight in my blind eye tonight when I go to the altar as I was sure of salvation when I went to the Methodist altar several years ago and was saved.* With this logical reasoning, she came to the altar, and while we were praying with others, she asked God to heal her. Before we had a chance to anoint her, she was on her feet weeping. She walked back and threw her arms around her father's neck. The audience wondered why she left the altar without being anointed. Her father said:

"What is the matter, daughter?" She replied, "My eye." He said: "Why, is it paining you?" She said: "No, I can see perfectly!"

A few months later, while we were holding a revival in St. Paul, Minnesota, we met this woman and her husband. They were there attending the Bible school, preparing for work for the Master. Her husband wanted to preach the Gospel of Christ, who had so graciously healed his wife.

Almost daily in our revivals, testimonies are given by those who have been healed while sitting in their seats listening to the Gospel.

What Eminent Men Have to Say

These views on healing in the Atonement are not new and peculiar only to myself. Many of the most godly and able teachers of the Church have seen and taught them. In addition to those teachers already quoted, I will add a few words from Dr. Torrey and others.

Dr. R. A. Torrey, in his book on "Divine Healing" declares:

The atoning death of Jesus Christ secured for us not only physical healing, but the resurrection and perfecting and glorifying of our bodies. . . . The Gospel of Christ has salvation for the body as well as for the soul. . . . Just as one gets the first-fruits of his spiritual salvation in the life that now is, so we get the first-fruits of our physical salvation in the life that now is. . . . Individual believers, whether Elders or not, have the privilege and the duty to "pray one for another" in case of sickness, with the expectation that God will hear and heal.

Dr. R. E. Stanton, a former moderator of the General Assembly of the Presbyterian Church, gives the following in his "Gospel Parallelisms":

It is my aim to show that the Atonement of Christ lays the foundation equally for deliverance from sin and for deliverance from disease. That complete provision has been made for both; that in the exercise of faith under the conditions prescribed, we have the same reason to believe that the body may be delivered from sickness that we have that the soul shall be delivered from sin; in short, that both branches of the deliverance stand on the same ground, and that it is necessary to include both in any true conception of what the Gospel offers to mankind. The atoning sacrifice of Christ covers the physical as well as the spiritual needs of the race. . . . Healing of the body is not, therefore, a "side-issue," as some represent it. It is no more this than the healing of the soul is a "side-issue." They are both but parts of the same Gospel, based equally upon the same great Atonement.

The following is the report of the Commission on Spiritual Healing appointed by the Episcopal Church. This was sponsored by Bishop Reese, who for many years has practiced the healing ministry and who was chairman of the commission. The commission states:

The healing of the body is an essential element of the Gospel, and must be preached and practiced. . . . God wills our health, that the Church, the "Body of Christ," has the same commission and the same power as "The Head," that we churchmen, with this true conception of God as Creative Love, must now give a sinning and suffering world this full Gospel of salvation from sin and its inevitable consequences.

These conclusions were arrived at by this scholarly commission after three years of study and research.

Bishop Charles H. Brent of the Episcopal Church was head of all chaplains in France and led the religious life of our armies overseas. He affirms: "He who waives away the healing power of Christ as belonging only to the New Testament times is not preaching the whole Gospel. God was, and is, the Savior of the body as well as the soul."

James Moore Hickson pleads: "A living Church is one in which the Living Christ lives and walks, doing through its members what He did in the days of His flesh. It must, therefore, be a *healing* Church as well as a soul-saving Church. . . . Spiritual healing is sacramental. It is the extension through the members of His mystical body of His own incarnate life."

The late able writers, Dr. A. B. Simpson, Andrew Murray, A. T. Pierson, Dr. A. J. Gordon and many present writers whom we might quote, have been teachers of healing in the Atonement. An unknown writer has said: "On the cross of Calvary Jesus has nailed the proclamation, *'Deliver him from going down to the pit (grave): I have found a ransom [an atonement]'* " (Job 33:24).

Isaiah begins the redemption chapter with the question, "Who hath believed our report? and to whom is the arm of the LORD revealed?" (Isaiah 53:1). And the report follows that He bore our sins and sicknesses. The answer to the question is, only those who have heard the report could believe it, because "faith cometh by hearing." Since Jesus died to save and to heal, it is surely worth reporting.

The purpose of this sermon is to prove that healing is provided by the Atonement and is therefore a part of the Gospel, which Christ commanded to be preached

> To "all the world,"
> To "all nations,"
> To "every creature,"
> With "all Power,"
> Throughout "all the days,
> Even unto the end of the age."

3

Is Healing for All?

Is it still the will of God, as in the past, to heal all who have need of healing, and to fulfill the number of their days?

The greatest barrier to the faith of many seeking bodily healing in our day is the uncertainty in their minds as to it being the will of God to heal *all*. Nearly everyone knows that God does heal *some*, but there is much in modern theology that keeps people from knowing what the Bible clearly teaches—that healing is provided for all. It is impossible to boldly claim, by faith, a blessing that we are not sure God offers. The power of God can be claimed only where the will of God is known.

It would be next to impossible to get a sinner to "believe unto righteousness" before you had fully convinced him that it was God's will to save *him*. Faith begins where the will of God is known. If it is God's will to heal only *some* of those who need healing, then none have any basis for faith unless they have a special revelation that they are among the favored ones. Faith must rest on the will of God alone, not on our desires or wishes. Appropriating faith is not believing that God *can* but that God *will*. Because of not knowing it to be a redemptive privilege for *all*, most of those in our day, when seeking healing, add to their petition the phrase, "If it be Thy will."

A Corrected Theology

Among all those who sought healing from Christ during His earthly ministry, we read of only one who had this kind of theology. This was the leper, who said, "Lord, *if Thou wilt*, Thou canst make me clean." The first thing Christ did was to correct his theology by saying, "*I will*, be thou clean." Christ's "I will" cancelled his "*if*." This added to his faith that Christ *could* heal him, the fact that He *would*.

The theology of this leper, before Christ enlightened him, is almost universal today, because this part of the Gospel is so seldom and so fragmentarily preached.

We see, from almost every conceivable angle throughout the Scriptures, that there is no doctrine more clearly taught than that it *is* God's will to heal all who have need of healing so that they may fulfill the number of their days according to His promise. Of course, we mean all who are properly taught and who meet the conditions prescribed in the Word. Now I hear someone say, "If healing is for all, then we shall never die." Why not? Divine healing goes no further than the promise of God. He does not promise that we shall never die, but He says:

> I will take sickness away from the midst of thee. . . . The number of thy days I will fulfil.
>
> Exodus 23:25, 26

The days of our years are threescore years and ten.

Psalm 90:10

Take me not away in the midst of my days.

Psalm 102:24

Why shouldest thou die before thy time?

Ecclesiastes 7:17

Then someone may ask, Well, how is a man going to die?

Thou takest away their breath, they die, and return to their dust.

Psalm 104:29

The Rev. P. Gavin Duffy writes on this point:

He has allotted to man a certain span of life, and His will is that life shall be lived out. I want you to recall that all those He called back from the dead were *young people* who had not lived out their fulness of years; and in that very fact we may well see His protest against premature death. . . . Of course, we must not expect that the old shall be physically young, but if the alloted span has not been spent we have a right to claim God's gift of health; and, even though it be past, if it be His Will that we should continue here for a time longer, it is equally His Will that we should do so in good health.

Death comes, and then we blame our God,
    And weakly say, "Thy will be done";
But never underneath the sod
    Has God imprisoned any one.
God does not send disease, or crime,
    Or carelessness, or fighting clans;
And when we die before our time,
    The fault is man's.

He is a God of life, not death;
    He is one God that gives us birth;
He has not shortened by a breath
    The life of any on the earth;
And He would have us dwell within
    The world our full allotted years.
So blame not God—for our own sin
    Makes our own tears.

                      Douglas Malloch

Read the Will and Know

If we would know what is in a will, let us read the will. If we want to know God's will on any subject, let us read His will. Suppose a lady should say, "My husband, who was very rich, has passed away; now, I wish I knew whether he left me anything in the will." I would say to her, "Why don't you read the will and see?"

The word *testament*, legally speaking, means a person's will. The Bible contains God's last will and testament, in which He bequeaths to us all the blessings of redemption. Since it is His "*last* will and testament," anything later is a forgery. A man never writes a new will after he is dead. If healing is in God's will for us, then to say that the age of miracles is past is virtually saying what is the opposite of the truth, that a will is no good after the death of the testator. Jesus is not only the testator, who died; He was resurrected and is also the Mediator of the will. He is our lawyer, so to speak. He will not cheat us out of the will, as some earthly lawyers do. He is our Representative at the right hand of God.

For the answer to the question under consideration, let us look away from modern tradition and go to the Word of God, which is a revelation of His will. The fifteenth chapter of Exodus typifies our redemption, and "was written for our admonition." Just after the passage of the Red Sea, God gave His first promise to heal. This promise was for *all*. God named the conditions, the conditions were met, and we read: "He brought them forth also with silver and gold, and there was not one feeble person among all their tribes." It is here that God gave the covenant of healing, revealed by and sealed with His first covenant and redemptive name, JEHOVAH-RAPHA, translated, "I am the LORD that healeth thee." This is God's Word, "settled in heaven," a never-changing fact concerning God.

Who Is Authorized to Change God's Will?

To say that this privilege of health is not for God's people today is to change God's "I *AM*" to "I *Was*" JEHOVAH-RAPHA. Who has the authority to change God's redemptive names? Instead of abandoning His office as Healer, He is "Jesus Christ the same yesterday, and today, and forever," under this first of seven covenant names. The blessings revealed by His redemptive names, as we have seen in the preceding sermon, were provided by the Atonement. He "tasted death *for every* man," and therefore cannot be confined to Israel. This fifteenth chapter of Exodus shows us that at least in that age of the world, 3,500 years ago, God did not leave the people in doubt concerning His willingness to heal *all*.

A Nation without One Feeble Person

This universal state of health in the nation of Israel continued as long as God's conditions were met. Twenty years later (Num. 16:46–50), when because of sin the plague destroyed 14,700, Israel again met the conditions. The plague was stayed, and He was still JEHOVAH-RAPHA the Healer, not to some, but to *all*. It would not be true that the plague was stayed if it remained on even one of them. This state of health again remained uninterrupted until nineteen years later. The people, not satisfied with God's way for them, chosen in love and mercy, spoke against God and against Moses. They were cursed with the fiery serpents. They again met God's conditions by confessing their sins. His Word through Moses to them was, "It shall come to pass, that *every one* that is bitten, when he looketh upon it [the brazen serpent, the type of Calvary], shall live" (21:8). Again, the Scriptures show us that it was still God's will to heal, not some, but *all*. *Everyone* that was bitten lived by beholding the brazen serpent, which was a typical foreshadowing of the coming sacrifice on Calvary in our behalf.

The psalmist David, in his time, understood healing to be a universal privilege. In the 86th Psalm he says, "For thou, Lord, art good, . . . plenteous in mercy unto *all* them that call upon thee." We shall see, in the following sermon, that healing was one of the most prominent mercies throughout the Scriptures. The sick, in the New Testament, asked for "mercy" when seeking healing from Christ. God's mercy covers man's physical, as well as spiritual, nature. Therefore, Jesus, according to the Old Testament promise, showed that He was "plenteous in mercy," by healing, not *some*, but *all* who came to Him. Again, in the 103rd Psalm, we see that David believed that the mercy of healing was as universal a privilege as the mercy of forgiveness. He calls on his soul to bless God, "Who forgiveth *all* thine iniquities, who healeth *all* thy diseases." "Who healeth *all*" is as permanent as "Who forgiveth *all*," for the identical language is used with reference to both mercies.

In Psalm 91:16, God says concerning the man "that dwelleth in the secret place of the most High": *"With long life will I satisfy him."* Is the privilege of dwelling in the secret place only for a few or for all? If it is for all, then God's promise to *all* is, "With long life will I satisfy him." God would have to break this promise to be unwilling to heal His obedient children living in middle life. If dwelling in the secret place was possible in a darker age of the world, surely it is possible in this better age of grace. "He is able to make all grace abound" toward each of His children today. The holy prophets of the Old Testament "prophesied of the grace that should come to *us.*"

Calvary Meets All Man's Needs

In the great redemption chapter, the 53rd chapter of Isaiah, it is *our* sicknesses, as well as *our* sins that Jesus bore. This makes one privilege as universal as the other. What Jesus did for individuals who came to Him for blessings was for *them*, but what He did on Calvary was for *all*.

It is clear that in all of these instances cited from the Old Testament, it was God's will to heal all who met the conditions. Wherever forgiveness was offered, healing was also offered. Let those who teach people that God's will in the matter of healing is not the same today, answer the question, "Why would God withdraw this Old Testament mercy from this better dispensation?" Is it not to be expected that He, who "hath reserved better things for us" and who is "the same yesterday, and today, and forever" should continue these same mercies throughout this better dispensation? Let us now look in the New Testament and see.

Christ, the Expression of God's Will

There is no better way of ascertaining the proper answer to the question before us than by reading the Gospels since they record the teachings and the works of Christ. He was the expression of the Father's will. His life was both a revelation and a manifestation of the unchanging love and will of God. He literally acted out the will of God for Adam's race. He said, "I came down from heaven, not to do my will, but the will of him that sent me." "The Father that dwelleth in me, he doeth the works." He also said, "He that hath seen me hath seen the Father." When He healed the multitudes who thronged Him, day after day, we see the Father revealing His will. When "he laid his hands on *every one* of them, and healed them," He was doing and revealing the will of God for *our* bodies. Perhaps no one would be more conservative than the scholars of the Episcopalian church. The appointed commission studied the subject of spiritual healing and reported back to the church. They spent three years of study and research in both the Bible and history. They said in their report, "The healing of the sick by Jesus was done as a revelation of God's will for man." Because they discovered that His will is fully revealed, they further said, "No longer can the Church pray for the sick with the *faith-destroying*, qualifying phrase 'If it be Thy will.' "

The message everywhere taught in the gospels is one of complete healing for soul and body for all who come to Him. Many today say, "I believe in healing, but I do not believe it is for everyone." If it is not, how could we pray the prayer of faith for anyone? Even if we pray for one whom it is God's will to heal, we must have a revelation by the Spirit that we are praying for the right one. If it is not God's will to heal *all*, then no man can ascertain the will of God for himself from the Bible. Are we to understand from these teachers that we must close our Bibles? Must we get our revelation directly from the Spirit, before we can pray for the sick, because the will of God cannot be ascertained from the Scriptures?

This would be virtually teaching that the whole of divine activity on the line of healing would have to be governed by the direct revelation of the Spirit, instead of by the Scriptures. How are the sick to be healed if there is no Gospel (good news) of healing to proclaim to them as a basis for their faith? Or, since faith is expecting God to keep His promise, how can there be faith for healing if there is no promise in the Bible that the sick can apply to himself? The Scriptures tell us how God heals the sick. "He sent his *word,* and healed them, and delivered them from their destructions" (Psalm 107:20). "the *word* of God, which effectually worketh" in them that believe is "health to all their flesh" (see 1 Thessalonians 2:13; Proverbs 4:22).

Faith Rests on More than Mere Ability

If a millionaire were to appear before an audience of a thousand people with the announcement that he was able to give each one a thousand dollars, this would be no basis for any to have faith for a thousand dollars. Faith cannot rest on ability. If he should go further, and say, "I will give fifty of you a thousand dollars each," even then there is no basis for anyone in the audience to have faith for the thousand dollars. Were you to ask one of them if he or she were "fully assured" of receiving a thousand dollars from the millionaire, the answer would be, "I need the money, and hope I am among the lucky ones, but I cannot be sure." But, should the millionaire say, "*It is my will* to give all a thousand dollars each," then everyone in the audience would have a ground for faith and would undoubtedly say to the rich man, "Thank you, I'll take my money."

Now, supposing God were a respecter of persons, and that it was His will to heal only *some* of those who need healing. Let us take a glance through the gospels and see how the friends of the sick decided which of the sick to bring to Him for healing. "Now when the sun was setting, *all* they that had *any* sick with divers diseases brought them unto him; and he laid his hands on *every one* of them, and healed them" (Luke 4:40). Here the unlucky ones, if there were any, were brought, and all healed the same as the others. Surely, it was God *doing* and *revealing* His own will. If you had been there and were sick, you would have been brought, and would have been healed with the rest, because they brought them *all*. Matthew, in his record of this same instance, tells why Jesus made no exceptions. He healed them all, "that it might be fulfilled which was spoken by Esaias, the prophet, saying, Himself took *our* infirmities, and bare *our* sicknesses." The word *our* means everybody, in the sacrifice of Calvary. It therefore requires the healing of *all*, to fulfill the prophecy. Not only on this occasion, but on every occasion until today, He heals the sick "that it might be fulfilled which was spoken by Esaias, the prophet, saying, Himself took *our* infirmities and bare *our* sicknesses."

Let the sick go through the gospels and note the *all*s and the *every*s and they will see that the redemptive blessing of healing was for *all*. No one ever appealed in vain to Jesus for healing. There never was a multitude large enough where Jesus wanted even one to remain sick and would not heal him.

Jesus Healed All Diseases

And Jesus went about all Galilee, teaching . . . and preaching the gospel . . . and healing *all manner* of sickness and *all manner* of disease among the people. And his fame went throughout all Syria: and they brought unto him all sick people that were taken with divers diseases and torments, and those which were possessed with devils, and those which were lunatick, and those that had the palsy; *and he healed them all* [Moffat's translation]. And there followed him great multitudes of people from Galilee, and from Decapolis, and from Jerusalem, and from Judaea, and from beyond Jordan.

Matthew 4:23–25

And Jesus went about all the cities and villages, teaching . . . and preaching the gospel . . . and healing *every sickness* and *every disease* among the people. But when he saw the multitudes, he was moved with compassion on them. . . . And when he had called unto him his twelve disciples, he gave them power against unclean spirits, to cast them out, and to heal *all manner* of sickness and *all manner* of disease.

Matthew 9:35–36; 10:1

Note that it was the multitudes coming for healing that necessitated the thrusting forth of new laborers into His harvest to preach and to heal. It was not long until seventy more were needed, and were sent forth to heal as well as to preach.

But when Jesus knew it, he withdrew himself from thence: and *great multitudes* followed him, *and he healed them all.*

Matthew 12:15

59

And Jesus went forth, and saw a *great multitude*, and was moved with compassion toward them, and he healed their sick.

Matthew 14:14

And when they were gone over, they came into the land of Gennesaret. And when the men of that place had knowledge of him, they sent out into all that country round about, and brought unto him *all that were diseased*; and besought him that they might only touch the hem of his garment: and as many as touched were made perfectly whole.

Matthew 14:34–36

And a *great multitude* of people out of all Judaea and Jerusalem, and from the sea coast of Tyre and Sidon, which came to hear him, and to be healed of their diseases; and they that were vexed with unclean spirits: and they were healed. And the *whole multitude* sought to touch him: for there went virtue out of him, and healed them *all*.

Luke 6:17–19

We see throughout the gospels that, in bringing the sick to Christ for healing, it was repeatedly stated that they brought them *all*, which included all the unlucky ones if there were any. If according to modern tradition, it is God's will for the sick to patiently remain so for His glory, is it not strange that there should not be even one of this class in all these multitudes brought to Christ for healing? By healing the epileptic (Mark 9:14–29) Jesus proved it to be the Father's will to heal even this one whom the disciples, divinely commissioned to cast out demons, failed to deliver. We see by this verse that it would have been wrong to call in question and to teach God's unwillingness to heal because of this failure on the part of the disciples. Jesus, by healing him, shows them that the failure proved nothing but unbelief. Peter, after three years of constant association with the Lord, describes His earthly ministry in this one brief statement: "God anointed Jesus of Nazareth with the Holy Ghost and with power: who went about doing good, and healing all that were oppressed of the devil; for God was with him" (Acts 10:38).

So, in all the above, and many other Scriptures that show He healed them *all*, we have the will of God revealed for our bodies, and the answer to the question, "Is healing for all?"

Compassionate Love—Jesus' Ruling Motive

Many, in our day, have been taught that Christ performed miracles of healing just to show His power and to prove His deity. This may be true, but it is far from being *all* the truth. He would not have had to heal *all* to show His power; a few outstanding cases would have proved this. But the Scriptures show that He healed because of His compassion and to fulfill prophecy. Others teach that He healed the sick to make Himself known, but in Matthew 12:15–16, we read, "Great multitudes followed him, and he healed them *all;* and charged them that they should *not make him known."*

Some, who have to admit that Jesus healed all who came to Him, hold that Isaiah's prophecy concerning His bearing our sicknesses refers only to His earthly ministry; that this universal manifestation of His compassion was special, and not a revelation of the unchanging will of God. But the Bible clearly teaches that He only *"began to do and teach"* what was not only to be continued, but augmented, after His ascension.

After Christ, for three years, had healed all that came to Him, He said, "It is expedient (profitable) for you that I go away." How could this be true if His going away would modify His ministry to the afflicted?

Anticipating the unbelief with which this wonderful promise would be regarded, He prefaced His promise to continue the same and greater works in answer to our prayers after His exaltation, with the words "verily, verily." "Verily, verily, I say unto you, he that believeth on me, the works that I do shall he do also; and greater works than these shall he do; because I go unto my Father. And [how are we to do them?] whatsoever ye shall ask in my name, that will I do, that the Father may be glorified in the Son" (John 14:12–13). In other words, we are to do them by asking Him to do them.

He did not say "less works," but "*the* works" and "*greater* works." To me, this promise from the lips of Christ is a complete answer to all opposers and to all their books and articles against divine healing.

"It is written" was Christ's policy when resisting the devil.

William Jennings Bryan well asked, "Since Christ said 'It is written,' and the devil said 'It is written,' why can't the preacher say 'It is written'?"

The Wisdom of the Early Church

The early Church took Christ at His Word and prayed unitedly for signs and wonders of healing, until "the place was shaken where they were assembled together." Then, "they brought forth the sick into the streets and laid them on beds and couches. . . . There came also a multitude out of the cities round about Jerusalem, bringing sick folks, and they which were vexed with unclean spirits, and they were *healed every one.*" "All that Jesus *began* to do and to teach" He was here continuing from the right hand of God through "His Body, the Church," according to His promise. Some say, "Oh, that was only in the beginning of the Acts, for the purpose of confirming their word regarding Christ's resurrection."

Let us turn to the *last* chapter of Acts and read how thirty years later, after Paul on the island of Melita had healed the father of Publius, "All the other sick people in the island came and were cured" (Weymouth).

In the very last chapter of the Acts of the Holy Ghost, which is the only unfinished book of the New Testament, it is still the will of God to heal; not some, but *all*.

The Acts of the Holy Ghost

The Holy Spirit, whom Christ sent as His Successor and Executive, took possession of the Church, which is the Body of Christ. He showed the same healing power *after* Pentecost that Christ had displayed *before*, and vast multitudes were healed. As in the gospels, so in the Acts, we never read of anyone asking for healing and being denied. Men have named this book the "Acts of the Apostles." A better and a truer name for this book would be "The Acts of the Holy Ghost." It records the acts of the Holy Ghost through others as well as the apostles. Philip and Stephen, who were not apostles, were as gloriously used as Peter and John. The Holy Spirit came to execute for us all the blessings purchased by Christ's redemption and pledged by the seven redemptive names. He has never lost any of His interest in the work He came to do. If you wish to know how He wants to act *today*, read how He did act. The book of Acts shows us how He wants to act throughout "all the days, even unto the end of the age."

It was the Holy Spirit who worked all the miracles of healing at the hands of Christ. Jesus never undertook a miracle until the Holy Spirit, the Miracle-Worker, came upon Him. Then, in full reliance on the Spirit, He cast out devils and healed the sick. The miracles of Christ were all done by the Spirit in advance of His own dispensation, or before He had yet entered officially into office. Why would the Holy Spirit, who healed all the sick before His dispensation began, do less after He entered office? Did the Miracle-Worker enter office to do away with miracles during His own dispensation?

Is the teaching and the practice of the Church in the matter of healing in this Laodicean (lukewarm) period of her history a truer expression of the will of God than the teaching and practice of the early Church while under the full sway of the Spirit? Decidedly not! I do not hesitate to say that modern theology has robbed the Holy Spirit of a part of His ministry.

Christ's Present Attitude

Now, in summing up what we have thus far written, we have a revelation from many angles of Christ's merciful attitude toward our sicknesses and infirmities since His exaltation at the right hand of God.

We deal now not with the past but only with Christ's *present* attitude toward sickness and disease.

1. Christ's present attitude is fully revealed by His redemptive name Jehovah-Rapha. His redemptive names cannot change. All will admit that His *other* six redemptive names are a revelation of His *present* attitude in the matter of bestowing the blessing that each name was given to reveal. By what logic can we suppose that He has abandoned His office as Healer, revealed by the name Jehovah-Rapha?
2. His present attitude is again fully revealed by His own definite promise to continue and augment His

healing ministry in answer to the prayer of believers while He is at the right hand of God. "Verily, verily, I say unto you, he that believeth on me, *the works* that I do shall he do also; and *greater works* than these shall he do, because I go unto my Father. And whatsoever ye shall ask in my name, that will I do, that the Father may be glorified in the Son" (John 14:12–13).

3. His present attitude is revealed by His own fulfillment of the above promise, recorded in the Book of Acts. Even in the very last chapter, thirty years after His ascension, we read, "*All* the other sick people in the island came and were cured" (Acts 28:9 Weymouth).

4. His present attitude is revealed by the fact that healing is a part of the Gospel of the Great Commission that Christ commanded to be preached. This commission is followed by the promise "they shall lay hands on the sick, and they shall recover" (Mark 16:15, 18).

5. His present attitude is revealed by the fact that His substitutionary work on Calvary was on behalf of all those who live on earth during His exaltation at the right hand of the Father. We have seen in the preceding sermon that, as in Leviticus, it is recorded that all disease was healed on the ground of Atonement. Matthew tells us that the Atonement was Christ's reason for making no exceptions in healing the sick who came to Him.

6. His present attitude is revealed by the plain command to "any sick" in the Church, while He is with the Father, to ask for anointing and prayer with the promise "the Lord shall raise him up" (James 5:14–15). Does He mean we shall pray with faith or without it? How can we pray "the prayer of faith" unless it is His will

to heal? Does He command us to pray for a thing He will not do? Right here, even laymen are commanded to confess their faults one to another and pray one for the other for healing, with the purpose that Elijah prayed for rain (James 5:16–18). Would God command us to thus intercede for what it is not His will to do? Certainly not!

7. His present attitude is revealed by the fact that it is since His exaltation that He "set" (established) in the Church teachers, miracles, gifts of healing, etc. This was for the continuance of the "same works" and "greater works," which He promised He would continue from God's right hand. History records the manifestation of these miraculous gifts since the days of the apostles down to the present time.

The Unchangeable Compassion of Jesus

8. His present attitude toward our sickness is wonderfully revealed by the fact that since His exaltation, His compassion has neither been withdrawn nor modified.

In a later sermon, on the subject of the Lord's compassion, we shall see that during the earthly ministry of our Lord He was everywhere "*moved with compassion* and healed *all* that had need of healing." The same Greek word that is translated "mercy" is also repeatedly translated "compassion," for they are the same. When two blind men asked for mercy, Jesus was moved with compassion and healed them.

Since bodily healing, in the New Testament, is everywhere a mercy (it being mercy, or compassion, that moved Him to heal all that came to Him), is not the promise still true that He is "plenteous in mercy unto *all* them that call" upon Him? Does not this glorious Gospel dispensation proffer as much mercy and compassion to its sufferers as did the darker dispensation? The Reverend Kenneth Mackenzie, a noted teacher and writer of the Episcopal Church, asks on this point, "Could the loving heart of the Son of God, Who had compassion upon the sick, and healed all who had need of healing, cease to regard the sufferings of His own when He had become exalted at the right hand of the Father?"

Is it not strange that anyone in this better age of grace should take a position that would be synonymous with saying that the manifestation of Christ's compassion to the afflicted has been withdrawn, or even modified, since His glorification? If God is not as willing to show the mercy of healing to His *worshipers* as He is to show the mercy of forgiveness to His *enemies*, then He is more willing to show mercy to the devil's children than His own. The Scriptures deny this by saying, "The mercy [compassion] of the Lord is from everlasting to everlasting [not upon the sinner alone, but] upon *them that fear Him.*" He loves His own sick and suffering child even more than He loves the sinner. Thank God "... His mercy [compassion] is everlasting; and his truth endureth to all generations."

Blessings for All

9. Christ's present attitude is revealed by the fact that in the Old Testament year of jubilee (Leviticus 25:28), which Jesus in Luke 4:19 applies to the Gospel era, it was *"every man"* who was told to return to his possession. In the year of jubilee its blessings were for *"every man."* In the Gospel era, its blessings are for *"every creature."* This is more fully developed in the preceding sermon.

10. His present attitude is also revealed by the fact that "He hath redeemed *us* (all of us) from the curse of the

law" (Galatians 3:13). We have seen in the preceding sermon that this curse included all the diseases known to history. How can God justify us and at the same time require us to remain under the curse from which He redeemed us?

The Earnest of Complete Redemption

11. His present attitude is revealed by the fact that the Holy Spirit and His work in us is "the earnest of our inheritance until the redemption of the purchased possession" (Ephesians 1:14). We have already pointed out that because our eternal destiny is both spiritual and bodily, our redemption must also be. Therefore we cannot receive our *full* inheritance until the coming Day of Redemption. But, thank God, by being filled with the Spirit, *we* now have the "*earnest*" of it. Paul tells us, we "*have* the firstfruits of the Spirit." These are manifested both spiritually and physically. The "firstfruits of the Spirit" include the earnest of immortality. This is a foretaste of the resurrection. Since our bodies are members of Christ, His glorified bodily life is as truly linked with our bodies, as His spiritual life is linked with our spirits. The same life that is in the vine is in its branches. In Christ, "the true vine," there is both spiritual and bodily life. It is only by bringing into our bodies some of the same life that He is to bring at the resurrection that the Spirit can be the earnest of our inheritance to the body. Since our inheritance includes a glorified body, what must the earnest be? Thank God, "the life also of Jesus" may "be made manifest in our mortal flesh." His *immortal* life touches our *mortal* bodies with a foretaste of redemption. This enables

us to finish our course in order that we may "receive a full reward."

12. Does not nature itself reveal the present attitude of Christ toward the healing of our bodies? Nature everywhere is healing, or at least doing her best to heal. As soon as disease germs enter our bodies, nature begins to expel them. Break a bone, or cut a finger, and nature will do her utmost to heal, and usually succeeds. Now, has God commanded nature to rebel against His own will? If sickness is the will of God for His children, would it not seem that He has?

Does God Use Bodily Affliction?

If sickness, as some think, is the will of God for His faithful children, then it is a sin for them even to desire to be well. This says nothing of spending thousands of dollars to defeat His purpose. I truly thank God for all the help that has ever come to sufferers through the physician, through the surgeon, the hospital and the trained nurse. If sickness is the will of God, then, to quote one writer, "Every physician is a lawbreaker; every trained nurse is defying the Almighty; every hospital is a house of rebellion, instead of a house of mercy." If this were true, instead of *supporting* hospitals, we ought to do our utmost to *close* every one.

If the modern theology of those who teach that God wants some of His worshipers to remain sick for His glory is true, then Jesus, during His earthly ministry, never hesitated to rob the Father of all the glory He could by healing *all* who came to Him. The Holy Spirit, likewise, robbed Him of all the glory He could by healing all the sick in the streets of Jerusalem. And Paul, too, robbed God of all the glory he could by healing *all* the sick on the island of Melita.

Many today hold that God afflicts even the obedient because He loves them, making sickness a love-token from our heavenly Father. If this is true, why do they try to get rid of His love-token? Why does not the one suffering with a cancer pray for a second blessing for themselves and also ask Him to thus bless their wife, children, father, mother, neighbors, etc.?

Does not God sometimes chasten His people through sickness? Decidedly yes! When we disobey God, sickness may be permitted, through the Father's loving discipline. But God has told us just how it may be avoided and averted. "If we would judge ourselves, we should not be judged. But when we are judged, we are chastened of the Lord, that we should not be condemned with the world" (1 Corinthians 11:31–32). These chastenings come to save us from final judgment. When we see the cause of the chastening, and turn from it, God promises it shall be withdrawn. As soon as "we judge ourselves," or learn our lesson, the absolute promise is "we shall not be judged." By self-judgment we may avoid chastening. Divine healing is not unconditionally promised to all Christians, regardless of their conduct. It is for those who believe and obey. "All the paths of the LORD are *mercy* and truth unto *such* as keep his covenant and his testimonies" (Psalm 25:10).

13. Our Lord's attitude now is shown by the fact that He was manifested to "destroy the works of the devil" (1 John 3:8). Think of His leaving heaven and making the awful transition of becoming a man, and of all the suffering and sacrifice that followed. What was the purpose that moved Him in all this? The Scriptures give the answer. "For *this* purpose . . . that He might destroy the works of the devil." This purpose includes

the healing of "*all* that were oppressed of the devil" (Acts 10:38). Since He was glorified, has He relinquished this purpose, which He retained even during the bloody sweat of Gethsemane and the awful tortures of Calvary? Does He want the works of the devil that He formerly wanted to destroy to remain in our bodies? Can it be that He now wants a cancer, a "plague," a "curse," "the works of the devil," in "the members of Christ," and "the temples of the Holy Ghost"? Is it not truly His will to heal any part of "the Body of Christ"? If not, why has He commanded "any sick" in it to be anointed *in His name* for healing?

Since "the Body is for the Lord," a "living sacrifice unto God," would He not rather have a well body than one that is a wreck? If not, how can He make us "perfect in every good work to do His will"? It is God's expressed will that we "may abound to every good work," that we may be "prepared unto every good work" "thoroughly furnished unto all good works," "zealous of good works" and "careful to maintain good works." Is this only for well men and women? If for all, He would have to heal the sick to make this possible. No man can "abound unto every good work" while confined to a sickroom.

Salvation All-Inclusive

14. His present attitude is revealed in the very meaning of the word *salvation*. The word *soteria*, which is the Greek word for salvation, implies deliverance, preservation, healing, health and soundness. In the New Testament it is applied sometimes to the soul and at other times to the body only. The Greek word *sozo* translated "saved" also means "healed," "made sound," "made whole." In Romans 10:9 it is translated "saved,"

and in Acts 14:9 the same word is translated "healed" in referring to the healing of the man lame from birth. Both Greek words for *salvation* and *saved* mean both spiritual and physical salvation, or in other words, spiritual and physical healing. Paul states in Ephesians 5:23 that "he is the saviour of the body."

Is this for some, or for all?

Dr. Scofield, in his footnote on the word *salvation* says, "Salvation is the great inclusive word of the Gospel, gathering into itself all the redemptive acts and processes." The word, therefore, includes our possession and enjoyment of all the blessings revealed by His seven redemptive names. These names were given to show what our *salvation* includes. It is therefore the Gospel of healing for the body, as well as for the soul, which "is the power of God unto salvation to *every one* that believeth; to the Jew first, and *also to the Greek.*" "The same Lord over *all* is rich unto *all* that call upon Him."

4

The Lord's Compassion

The LORD is gracious, and full of compassion; slow to anger, and of great mercy. The LORD is good to all: and his tender mercies are over all his works.

Psalm 145:8–9

In the study of the Lord's compassion, we have a complete revelation of the Lord's willingness to heal. During His earthly ministry He was everywhere moved with compassion, and healed all "them that had need of healing." It is "this same Jesus" who, after saying, "It is expedient for you that I go away," is now seated at the right hand of God, "that He might be a merciful [compassionate] and faithful High Priest" for us.

In the Scriptures, *compassion* and *mercy* mean the same. The Hebrew noun *rachamin* is translated both "mercy" and "compassion." The Greek verb *eleeo* is translated "have mercy" and "have compassion"; and likewise, the Greek adjective *eleemon* is defined "merciful-compassionate."

To have compassion is to love tenderly, to pity, to show mercy, to be full of eager yearning.

God's Greatest Attribute Is Love

The text above begins with, "The LORD is gracious, and full of compassion." These sentiments concerning the nature of God are expressed over and over throughout the Scriptures. God's greatest attribute is love—this is connected to His Fatherhood. The most conspicuous statements in the Scriptures about our heavenly Father are the declarations concerning His love, His mercy, His compassion. There is no note that can be sounded concerning God's character that will so inspire faith as this one. In our revivals, I have seen faith rise "mountain high" when the truth of God's present love and compassion began to dawn on the minds and hearts of the people. It is not what God can do, but what we know He *yearns* to do, that inspires faith.

By showing His compassion everywhere in the healing of the sick, Jesus unveiled the compassionate heart of God to the people. The multitudes came to Him for help. How insidiously Satan has worked to hide this glorious fact from the people. He has broadcasted the unscriptural, illogical, and worn-out statement that the age of miracles is past, until he has almost succeeded in eclipsing the compassion of God from the eyes of the world. Modern theology magnifies the *power* of God more than it magnifies His *compassion*; His power more than it does the great fact that "the exceeding greatness of His power [is] to *usward*." But the Bible reverses this and magnifies His willingness to use His power more than it does the power itself. In no place does the Bible say that "God is power," but it *does* say that "God is *love*." It is not faith in God's *power* that secures His blessings, but faith in His *love* and in His will.

God's Love Veiled by Modern Theology

The first statement in our text above is, "The LORD is gracious," meaning "He is disposed to show favors." This glorious fact, which shines with such brilliancy throughout the Scriptures, has been so eclipsed by modern theology that we hear everywhere, the Lord is *able* instead of "the LORD is *gracious.*" Hundreds needing healing have come or written to us saying, concerning their need of deliverance, "the Lord is able." Their teachings, as well as their lack of teaching, have kept them from knowing that the Lord is *willing.* How much faith does it take to say the Lord is able? The *devil* knows God is able, and he knows He is willing; but he has kept the *people* from knowing the latter fact. Satan is willing that we shall magnify the Lord's power, because he knows that this is not a sufficient basis for faith, but that the Lord's compassion and willingness are.

Before praying for the healing of people, we have to wait to teach them the Word of God until they can say, "The LORD is gracious," instead of, "The Lord is willing." This is exactly what Jesus had to do before healing the leper who said, "If thou wilt thou canst." He showed His willingness, so that the man could really expect healing.

In the preceding sermon, we have presented many scriptural proofs of the Lord's present willingness to heal. But even when we can advance from saying "He is able" to saying "He is willing," this is not enough. The word *willing* is too tame to fully express God's merciful attitude toward us. "He *delighteth* in mercy" (Micah 7:18). We have His attitude more fully expressed in 2 Chronicles 16:9, "For the eyes of the LORD run to and fro throughout the whole earth, to shew himself strong in the behalf of them whose heart is perfect toward him." This text exhibits our Lord as not only being *willing*, but *eager* to pour His blessings in great profusion upon all who make it possible for Him to do so. "For the eyes of the LORD run to and fro," or in other words, He is ever hunting for opportunities to gratify His benevolent heart, because "He *delighteth* in mercy."

Benevolence is the great attribute of God. If you want to please Him, remove the obstacles out of the way of the exercise of His benevolence. He is infinitely good. He exists forever in a state of entire consecration to pour forth blessings upon His creatures whenever they make it possible. Everyone can do this. Suppose the vast Pacific Ocean were elevated high above us. Then conceive of its pressure into every crevice to find an outlet through which it might pour its ocean tides over all the earth. You have a picture of God's benevolent attitude toward us.

A Serious Challenge

After first being properly enlightened, I challenge you, Reader, to place yourself where God's mercy can reach you without His having to violate the glorious principles of His moral government. Then wait and see if you don't experience the most overwhelming demonstration of His love and mercy. The blessing will flow until you have reached the limit of your expectation. Cornelius placed himself where God's mercy could reach him by saying to Peter, "We are all here present before God to hear all things that are commanded thee of God." He found God's goodness so great that He could not wait for Peter to finish his sermon. Just as soon as Peter had spoken enough to be a basis for their faith, down came the blessing.

Not only is God *able,* but He is also *willing* to do "exceeding abundantly above all that we ask or think." His love is so great that it could not be fully gratified by blessing all the holy beings in the universe. Therefore, it is extended to His enemies "throughout the whole earth." It seems to me that God would rather have us doubt His ability than His willingness. I would rather have a man who is in trouble say to me, "Brother Bosworth, I know you would help me if you could" (doubting my ability) than to say, "I know you can, but I have no confidence in your disposition to help me."

Again, the text at the head of this sermon further states that the Lord is "full of compassion; slow to anger, and of great mercy." When I think of how the Lord so floods *our* hearts with His tender love, until, in intercession for others, our hearts are too full of yearnings to utter their feelings (yearnings that "cannot be uttered"), I stand in awe, and wonder what *His* compassion must be. A mother's compassion for her suffering child makes her not only willing to relieve the child, but to suffer if she cannot. The Greek word *sumpathes* (translated "compassion") means to suffer with another. Accordingly Isaiah says: "In all their affliction he was afflicted." Is it not strange that this wondrous fact of His mercy toward the sick, so clearly seen and applied during the darker ages of the Old Testament, should be overlooked and set aside in this "better" age? Christ has opened the way for the fullest possible manifestations of His mercy toward every phase of human need.

The Benevolent Heart of God Reaches All

Our text, after showing the greatness of His compassion, closes with the logical conclusion, "The LORD is good to *all*: and his tender mercies are over *all* his works." In other words, He is so "full of compassion" that He cannot be "a respecter of persons" in the bestowal of His mercies. God is unable to fully gratify His benevolent heart by blessing holy beings. He has to extend His mercies to the wicked of earth. How could He withhold the common blessing of healing from any of His *own* obedient children?

Prophets and kings desired to see, and angels desired to look into this age of grace. What a strange doctrine that the sick are not to look for as much mercy during this time of light as sufferers did during the darker ages. Is God now more willing to show the mercy of forgiveness to the devil's children than He is the mercy of healing to His own? The fact is, He loves His own sick and suffering child even more than He loves the sinner. "The mercy [compassion] of the LORD is from everlasting to everlasting [not upon sinners alone, but] upon *them that fear Him.*" "Like a father pitieth *his* children, so the LORD pitieth them that fear him." "As the heaven is high above the earth, so great is his mercy toward them that fear him," as well as to the sinner. The sick Christian can say, with Solomon, ". . . there is no God like thee . . . which keepest covenant, and sheweth mercy *unto thy servants,* that walk before thee with all their hearts" (2 Chronicles 6:14). Not some, but "*All* the paths of the LORD are *mercy* and truth [not unto His enemies, but] *unto such as keep his covenant* and his testimonies" (Psalm 25:10).

Instances of the Lord's Compassion

Let us look at a few passages from the gospels, showing the Lord's compassion.

> And there came a leper to him, beseeching him, and kneeling down to him, and saying unto him, If thou wilt, thou canst make me clean. And Jesus, *moved with compassion,* put forth

his hand, and touched him, and saith unto him, I will; be thou clean. And as soon as he had spoken, immediately the leprosy departed from him, and he was cleansed. . . . And they came to him from every quarter.

Mark 1:40–45

Here it was compassion that moved Christ to heal this leper.

He departed thence by ship into a desert place apart: and when the people had heard thereof, they followed him on foot out of the cities. And Jesus went forth, and saw a great multitude, and *was moved with compassion* toward them, and he healed their sick.

Matthew 14:13–14

Here, as elsewhere, He was "plenteous in mercy" to "all that had need of healing." It was His compassion that moved Him.

And as they departed from Jericho, a great multitude followed him. And, behold, two blind men sitting by the wayside, when they heard that Jesus passed by, cried out, saying, Have *mercy* on us, O Lord, thou Son of David. . . . And Jesus . . . said, What will ye that I shall do unto you? They say unto him, Lord, that our eyes may be opened. So Jesus *had compassion* on them, and touched their eyes: and immediately their eyes received sight, and they followed him.

Matthew 20:29–34

These blind men asked for the mercy of having their eyes opened. Jesus granted them the mercy of healing, proving that healing is a mercy as well as forgiveness. The sick, in those days, when seeking *healing*, asked for *mercy*. In our day most people think of mercy as applied only to the sinner, not knowing that His mercy is also extended to the sick.

God the Father of Mercies

Paul, who calls God the "Father of mercies," proves it by healing all the sick on the island of Melita. Jesus said, "Blessed are the merciful [compassionate]: for they shall obtain mercy." Job was healed when he prayed for his friends. According to one of the beatitudes, he obtained mercy by showing it. Referring to and accounting for Job's healing, James 5:11 says, "The Lord is very pitiful, and of tender mercy." He follows with the direction to the Church: "Is *any sick* among *you*? let him call for the elders of the church," etc. "The Lord is very pitiful, and of tender mercy." In other words, let "any sick" in the Church today, as well as Job, obtain their healing also. Jesus provided all we need. He is still saying, as He did to the two blind men, "What will ye that I should do unto you?"

Jesus had compassion on the man in the tombs. The man was so possessed with a legion of demons that he cut himself with stones and broke the chains with which people had often tried to bind him. When he was clothed and in his right mind, he was so glad that he besought the Lord that he might remain with Him. "Howbeit Jesus suffered him not, but saith unto him, Go home to thy friends, and tell them how great things the Lord hath done for thee, and hath had *compassion* on thee. And he departed, and began to *publish* in Decapolis how great things Jesus had done for him: and all men did marvel" (Mark 5:19–20).

A Result of One Man's Testimony

Let us read Matthew 15:30–31, and see the results of this one man's testimony given to advertise the Lord's compassion.

And great multitudes [in Decapolis] came unto him, having with them those that were lame, blind, dumb, maimed, and many others, and cast them down at Jesus' feet; and he healed them: insomuch that the multitude wondered, when they saw the dumb to speak, the maimed to be whole, the lame to walk, and the blind to see: and they glorified the God of Israel.

It was not their being sick, as some teach today, but their being healed that caused these "great multitudes" to "glorify the God of Israel." Oh, how much glory would come to God, as well as blessings to the world, if every minister today would present clearly the Bible promises for healing to the sick. What blessing there would be if, as soon as each one was healed, he would publish the Lord's compassion throughout his "Decapolis." In a short time thousands upon thousands everywhere who are now sick would obtain faith in Christ for healing. It would then again be said of the multitudes that they "glorified the God of Israel." The higher critic and the modernist would soon be unpopular, and the false healing cults would not draw away from the Church the multitudes who are now being ensnared.

It is stated above that this man "published" the Lord's compassion. Some oppose and write articles against us for publishing the testimonies of those who are miraculously healed. What is the matter? Is there anything wrong in obeying the Lord's command to "make known *his* deeds among the people?" Since Jesus died to open the way for His mercies to reach all the needs of man, we surely ought to be willing for them to know it. One would think, to read some of the books and articles that are being written, that it is a crime to let the people know about the Lord's compassion.

You will notice that in the Scriptures quoted above, as the result of miracles of healing, Jesus' fame was spread abroad, "and *they came to him from every quarter.*" And "they followed him on foot out of the cities," and "great multitudes came unto him." "Multitudes!" "Multitudes!" "Multitudes," everywhere.

It is the same today. As the command is obeyed to "make known his deeds among the people" and His compassion is "published," things begin to happen. As soon as it is known in any city that "this same Jesus" is actually healing the sick, people come "from every quarter." I have never seen anything that will so break down all the barriers, and bring the people from every quarter, as the manifestation of the Lord's compassion in healing the sick. We have found in our revivals that as soon as the public find out what "this same Jesus" is doing, they come from every quarter. They come from the Methodist quarter, from the Baptist quarter, from the Catholic quarter, from the Christian Science quarter, from the Unity quarter, from the Spiritist quarter, from the Jewish quarter, from the poor man's quarter, from the rich man's quarter and from every quarter. Multitudes hear the Gospel and give their lives to God. They would never even attend the meetings if there were no healing miracles to reveal His compassion.

The Effect of Present-day Healings

If Christ and His apostles could not draw the multitudes without miracles, does He expect more from us? We preached for thirteen years before the Lord led us to preach this part of the Gospel in a bolder and more public way. Instead of the "ministry of healing" diverting from the more important matter of salvation for the soul, we have seen more happy conversions in a single week than we ever saw in a whole year of evangelistic work before. As soon as our revivals get under way, hundreds nightly crowd forward to give their hearts and lives to God. Whole cities begin talking about Jesus. Other evangelists who have visited our revivals are now proving this to be true in their own meetings.

Our last revival, preceding the writing of this book, was conducted in Ottawa, Canada. During the seven weeks of the meeting, six thousand came for healing, and about twelve thousand for salvation. I doubt if there would have been more than one thousand for salvation had it not been for the miracles of healing, which displayed the compassion of the Lord. The city and country were stirred as never before in its history. The largest crowds that ever gathered under one roof for religious meetings in this capital of Canada, filled the newly built million-dollar auditorium. This is the largest building in the city. The attendance ran as high as ten thousand in a single service. Before leaving the city, many hundreds of written testimonies were received. Those healed from almost every kind of disease and affliction told of what God had done. To God be all the glory!

One Baptist evangelist, who, among other evangelists, has now proved this to be true, has written in one of ten pamphlets he has published on the subject that **healing is the greatest evangelizing agency that the Lord ever used.** He said that he would not return to the old way (new way) for all the money in America.

The Increasing Harvest

Now let us look at another passage concerning the Lord's compassion.

And Jesus went about all the cities and villages, teaching in their synagogues, and preaching the gospel of the kingdom, and healing every sickness and every disease among the people. But when he saw the multitudes, he was *moved with compassion on them,* because they fainted, and were scattered abroad, as sheep having no shepherd. Then saith he unto his disciples, The harvest truly is plenteous, but the labourers are few; pray ye *therefore* the Lord of the harvest, that he will send forth labourers into his harvest. And when he had called unto him his twelve disciples, he gave them power against unclean spirits, to cast them out, and to heal all manner of sickness and all manner of disease . . . and commanded them, saying Go . . . preach . . . heal the sick.

Matthew 9:35–10:8

Here, Jesus' compassion toward the sick is now becoming so well known that the "harvest" has become too great for the ONE REAPER. His compassionate heart is full of yearning over the increasing numbers who could not reach Him because of the press. "When he saw the multitudes, he was moved with compassion on them." It is as though He was able to personally minister to but a portion of them, and His compassion for the rest of the rapidly growing multitudes is now moving Him to thrust forth other laborers to heal and preach. "*His* harvest" is not only the same in character in our day, but it is also much greater than when He was here. His compassion is still the same. He wants the same kind of reapers today to reap the same harvest by preaching and healing in "all the cities and villages." His compassion, manifested through these twelve new laborers, soon necessitated the thrusting forth of seventy more empowered to preach and to heal. Laborers of this kind are few today. "The harvest" truly is plenteous beyond what it was then. What He was beginning "to do and to teach" is exactly what He wants done and taught everywhere today. Instead of *ending* something, according to the modern idea, He was *starting* something, which He promised to continue and increase. It is not the twentieth-century Gospel, but "*this* Gospel" (the one that He proclaimed) that He said "shall be preached in all the world."

A Strange Reversal of Christ's Promise

Jesus, in John 14:12–13, emphatically taught and promised that the same mercy and compassion could reach the people through our prayers while He is our High Priest in Heaven. In fact, His departure was to open the way for His compassion to be manifested on a much larger scale. Isaiah prophesied of Him, "Therefore will he be exalted that he may have mercy." Jesus said, "It is expedient [profitable] for you that I go away." This could not be true if His going away would withdraw or even modify the manifestation of His compassion in healing the sick. Is it not strange that many ministers today exactly reverse Christ's promise, that the same and greater works shall be done, by teaching that the age of miracles is past? Others do the same by teaching that God wants some of His devout children to remain sick for His glory, as well as many other traditional and unscriptural ideas.

Every man who teaches that healing is not for all who need it today as it was in the past is virtually teaching that Christ's compassion toward the sick has been at least modified since His exaltation. Worse yet, others teach that His compassion in healing the sick has been entirely withdrawn. To me, it is a mystery how any minister can take a position that veils and interferes with the manifestation of the greatest attribute of deity. God's compassion is divine love in action. When Paul made the strongest possible appeal for consecration, he said, "I beseech you . . . by the *mercies* of God." This is the manifestation of His greatest attribute.

Our High Priest

Jesus said, "When he, the Spirit of Truth is come, . . . he shall glorify me." Could the Spirit glorify Christ to the sick by telling them that the age of miracles is past? He promised to do *"these* works . . . and greater works" during this age. Would it glorify Jesus if since His exaltation, He withdrew or modified His ministry to the sick? Has the Spirit come to magnify Christ by modifying His ministry to His sick and suffering brethren? Is Christ their High Priest? Would this be directly contrary to the glorifying of the God of Israel in Decapolis, occasioned by the healing of the multitudes? Are we to abandon our prayer of faith for our healing? If so, then the common practice of praying for the sick to have fortitude and patience to bear their affliction is right. Something is wrong!

It is since Jesus became our High Priest that He speaks from heaven seven times, saying, "He that hath an ear, let him hear what the Spirit saith unto the churches." Men are saying much today that the Spirit has *never* said and is the opposite of what He *does* say. The following are a few of the things the Spirit says for the purpose of glorifying Christ.

"Wherefore in all things it behoved him to be made like unto his brethren, that he might be a merciful [compassionate] and faithful *high priest"* (Hebrews 2:17). We have already shown that both the words *merciful* and *compassionate* are given as the meaning of the Greek adjective *eleemon* translated "merciful" in this passage. This verse has no reference to Christ's compassion as manifested during His earthly ministry. It refers only to His ministry from heaven, and to the fact that His incarnation was to the end that He might show compassion as our High Priest after His return to heaven. "All that Jesus began to do and teach until the day he was taken up" is what, because of His unchanging compassion, He promised would continue and be greater after He went away.

The Spirit further glorifies Christ by saying that He is *now* "touched [Greek, *sumpatheo*, translated "had compassion" in Hebrews 10:34] with the feeling of our infirmities." He still "can have compassion" (Hebrews 5:2). He is "Jesus Christ the same yesterday, and today, and forever." Let us worship Him, because His compassion is the same today. As He looks upon all our infirmities, He is still "moved with compassion" and yearns to help us.

We recognize that many who do not believe in divine healing *do* cooperate with the Spirit in these glorious sentiments as pertaining to the more important work of soul-saving. Some say that the age of miracles is past. While fulfilling His office-work of glorifying the exalted Christ, the Spirit expresses the deep sentiments of Hebrews 10:34. How wonderful it would be if all ministers and Christians would cooperate with the Spirit by also proclaiming these glorious sentiments to those suffering physically. Instead of being priests and Levites passing by on the other side, the Church, in James 5, is commanded to be a "good Samaritan." It must compassionately minister to the physical needs of the sick and afflicted. It should be binding up their wounds, pouring in the healing balm of wine and oil (the *Word* of God and the *Spirit* of God). "He sent his word, and healed them" by the power of the Spirit. Jesus pronounced a woe upon the scribes and Pharisees for having omitted the weightier matters of *mercy* and faith.

In the fifth chapter of Acts we have another wonderful proof that Christ's compassion toward the sick is now the same. We read concerning the multitudes brought into the streets of Jerusalem in the days after He had ascended to the Father, that "they were *healed every one*." Here it was again, as our High

Priest *in Heaven*, that Jesus did exactly what He did before going away. From heaven He was "moved with compassion, and healed all who had need of healing."

Even in the last chapter of Acts, we find His compassion manifested from heaven by the healing of all on the island of Melita. While He is our High Priest, His compassion is so great that "He ever liveth to make intercession for us."

Again, His compassion for the sick, since He was glorified, moved Him to "set" (establish) in the Church spiritual gifts. The gifts of faith, of miracles and of healing for the recovery of the sick are given through the centuries while He is our High Priest. Rev. W. C. Stevens says of these days following Christ's exaltation: "We find, as a matter of course and *of necessity*, 'gifts of healing,' taking just such rank and prominence as they did in our Lord's personal ministry on earth."

Even Laymen May Pray for the Sick

It is His present compassion for the sick that caused Jesus, as our High Priest and Head of the Church, to command the elders and even the laymen to pray the prayer of faith for the healing of "any sick" during the Church Age (James 5:14; Mark 16:17–18). Rev. W. C. Stevens on this point remarks, "All preachers, teachers, writers and others who hand out the Word of Life to the people, should keep this direction [James 5:14] as continuously before the people as sickness itself constantly confronts them."

Even during His earthly ministry, our adorable Lord would make any sacrifice and suffer even the curse, in order to open the way for His compassion to reach the most unworthy and the most provoking of His enemies. Both the bloody sweat of Gethsemane and the horrible tortures of Calvary were but the manifestations of His infinite compassion. He went to

Calvary with "His face set like flint." He had been betrayed
by the kiss of Judas into the hands of His crucifiers. Peter had
cut off the ear of the servant of the High Priest. Jesus heals
the ear of His enemy, and tells Peter to put up his sword. He
sheathed, as it were, His own sword, by holding in check the
most natural impulse of His holy soul. He refused to pray
when, by praying, He could have instantly had more than
twelve legions of angels to enable Him to escape the agony
of the cross. Then there would have been only a judgment
seat and no mercy seat. Fallen man with all his needs of
body, soul and spirit would have had no hope. In His substitutionary work for us He anticipated every possible need of
Adam's race, and opened the way for mercy to reach every
phase of human need. He was then, and is now, moved with
compassion toward all who need His help. The seven blessings of His covenant, His "Presence" as "Provider," "Peace,"
"Victory," "Shepherd," "Righteousness" and "Physician," are
secure because of the tragedy of His cross. They are revealed
to us by His redemptive names. His covenants, including the
covenant of healing, are given because of His mercy. "[He]
keepeth covenant and mercy with them that love him . . . to
a thousand generations" (Deuteronomy 7:9).

How Not to Grieve the Heart of Jesus

Doubting or ignoring His love and compassion grieves the
heart of Jesus. It made Him weep over Jerusalem. So many
times ministers have said in these days that we do not need
miracles now. They think of miracles only as signs to prove
the Lord's deity, etc. I have said to them, "If you had a cancer
eating your head off, you would need a miracle, would you
not?" Most people today are so in the dark on this subject
that it never occurs to them that there is mercy also for the

sick. They never think of the gifts of healing and miracles as being the manifestation of Christ's compassion. Hour after hour, and day after day, for three years, He healed all who came to Him *because of His compassion.* Are not the needs of sufferers today the same as they were in that day? Do they not need as much compassion as in the past?

We think of the countless numbers in despair, suffering with such intense agony that death would be a mercy. The physicians, after doing their best, have been obliged to say, "I can do no more for you." Christ's compassion, every moment, is still precisely as when it was manifested during the three years of His earthly ministry of love. How precious it is to know this as a fact upon which we may absolutely rely.

We have shown that bodily healing is a *mercy* that Christ everywhere bestowed upon all who sought it. He was the expression of the Father's will. We have the plain declarations, the Lord is "plenteous in *mercy* unto *all* them [including the sick] that call" upon Him because His mercy "endureth forever." His mercy is "from everlasting to everlasting." He is "full of mercy" "over *all* his works." Do not these Scriptures settle the matter? Instead of saying that the age of miracles is past, say, "It is written! It is written!"

5

How to Appropriate
the Redemptive and Covenant
Blessing of Bodily Healing

Note: In this sermon we are repeating a few of the statements made in the previous pages in order that this one sermon shall contain enough truth to lay a complete foundation for faith. This is done for the benefit of some who may need the prayer of faith for their healing before they have time to read the entire book.

The First Step

The first step toward being healed is the same as the first step toward salvation, or any other blessing that God promises. The sick person needs to know what the Bible clearly teaches and that it *is* God's will to heal until one has lived out the allotted span of life (seventy years, Psalm 90:10). Each individual sufferer must be convinced by the Word of God that his or her healing is the will of God. It is impossible to have real faith for healing as long as there is the slightest doubt as to it being God's will.

It is impossible to boldly claim by faith a blessing that we are not certain God offers. The power of God can be claimed only where the *will of God is* known. For instance, it would be next to impossible to get a sinner to "believe unto righteousness" before you had fully convinced him that it was God's will to save him. Faith begins where the will of God is known. Faith must rest on the will of God alone, not on our desires or wishes. Appropriating faith is not believing that God *can,* but that He *will.* Those who claim to believe in healing, but say one word in favor of it and ten words against it, cannot produce faith for healing.

Faith Is Expecting God to Do His Will

When God commands us to pray for the sick, He means for us to pray with faith. We could not do this if we did not know His will in the matter. Until a person knows God's will, he or she has no basis for faith. Faith is expecting God to do what we know it is His will to do. It is not hard, when we have faith, to get God to do His will.

When we know it is His will, it is not difficult for us to believe that He will do what we are sure He wants to do. It is in this way that every saved person has experienced the still greater miracle of the new birth. There can be no appropriation by faith until we are made to know by the Gospel what God has provided for us.

There is no doctrine more emphatically taught throughout the Word of God than that through the Atonement of Christ both salvation and bodily healing were provided. It is God's will to take away the sickness of those that serve Him, and to fulfill the number of their days according to His promise

(Exodus 23:25–26). As the types in Leviticus 14 and 15 show that it was *invariably* through *atonement* that sickness was healed under the law of Moses, so Matthew 8:17 definitely states that Jesus healed all diseases on the ground of the Atonement. This Scripture shows us that Christ's reason for making no exceptions while healing the sick who thronged Him was His Atonement. He made His Atonement for all Adam's race, including you. As multitude after multitude pressed upon Him "to hear Him and to be healed of their diseases," it is repeatedly stated throughout the gospels, "He healed them all" (read Matthew 4:24; 12:15; 14:14; Luke 4:40; Acts 10:38). He could make no exceptions. Why? Because in His coming Atonement, He "Himself took *our* infirmities." Since it is "*our*" infirmities He bore, it requires the healing of *all* to fulfill this prophecy. God carefully put this in such simple language that we would have to misquote it to leave ourselves out. **What Calvary provides is for all!**

God's way of saving the soul, of healing the body and of doing everything else He wants to do is to send His Word, His promise. He then keeps the promise wherever it produces faith. The divine procedure in healing is stated in the text, "He sent his word, and healed them, and delivered them from their destructions" (Psalm 107:20).

It is "the *word* of God, which effectually worketh" in them that believe. It is "health to all their flesh" (1 Thessalonians 2:13; Proverbs 4:22).

Just as a little girl's faith for a new dress comes by hearing the promise of her mother to buy it next Saturday, so our faith for healing comes by hearing God's Word. This is His promise that He will do it. Both the little girl's faith and ours "cometh by hearing." The little girl could not, and would not be expected to have faith for the new dress until her mother promised it. So we cannot, nor are we expected to, have faith for healing or salvation or any other blessing, until that faith comes by hearing the Word (the promise) of God to do it.

How could anyone find "justification by faith" until it was preached to him? How could anyone find healing by faith until it was preached to him? It is the Scriptures that are able to make men wise unto salvation. We must see that the Creator and Redeemer of the body is also its Physician before we can have reason to expect healing.

The Value of God's Redemptive Names

Since He heals us by sending His Word, what can be more His Word than His *redemptive* and covenant names, which were given, all seven of them, for the specific purpose of revealing to every man in Adam's race His redemptive attitude toward them?

When Christ commands us to "preach the Gospel to every creature," He means that we shall tell the "Good News" of redemption. His seven *redemptive* names reveal what our *redemption* includes. He has many other names, but only seven *redemptive* names. These seven names are never used in the Scriptures except in His dealings with man. Not six names, not eight, but seven, the perfect number, because He is a perfect Savior. His redemption covers the whole scope of human need. The blessings revealed by each of these names are all in the Atonement. For instance, JEHOVAH-SHAMMAH means "the LORD is present," "made nigh by the blood of Christ."

JEHOVAH-SHALOM is translated "the LORD is our Peace." This is in the Atonement because "the chastisement of our peace was upon him."

JEHOVAH-RA-AH is translated "the LORD is my Shepherd." He became our Shepherd by giving His life for the sheep. This privilege is in the Atonement.

94

JEHOVAH-JIREH means "the LORD will provide" an offering. Christ Himself was the offering provided on Calvary.

He became JEHOVAH-NISSI, "The LORD our Banner" or Victor, by spoiling principalities and powers on the cross.

He bore our sins, and became JEHOVAH-TSIDKENU, "the LORD our Righteousness." He opened the way for every sinner to receive the gift of righteousness.

JEHOVAH-RAPHA is translated "I am the LORD that healeth thee," or, "I am the LORD thy Physician." This also is in the Atonement, for He "himself took our infirmities and bare our sicknesses."

This completes the list of seven names, which were given for the purpose of revealing God's relationship toward all of us under each of these seven titles. These seven names all belong abidingly to Christ. It is under each of these seven titles that He "is the same yesterday, and today, and forever." Jesus says to all who come to Him for any of these seven blessings, "He that cometh unto me I will in no wise cast out."

This is the Good News that God wants preached to every creature, so that every creature may have the privilege of enjoying "the fullness of the blessing of the Gospel of Christ."

I say again that nothing is more God's Word "settled in heaven" than His redemptive name Jehovah-Rapha. No one has a right to change God's "I AM" Jehovah-Rapha to "I *was*." The "Word of the LORD endureth forever."

Since Jehovah-Shalom, "The LORD our Peace," is one of Christ's redemptive names, has not every man a redemptive right to obtain peace from Him? Has not every man, likewise, a redemptive right to obtain victory from Jehovah-Nissi? Has not every man a redemptive right to obtain "the gift of righteousness" from Jehovah-Tsidkenu, etc.? If so, why has not every man a redemptive right to obtain healing from Jehovah-Rapha?

This word Jehovah-Rapha was so accepted and believed by those to whom it was first sent that "there was not a feeble person among all their tribes." Whenever this state of health was interfered with by their transgressions, as soon as they repented, typical atonements were made. God was still Jehovah-Rapha *the Healer*, not to some, but to all. God wants this redemptive name, as well as all others, to be sent "to every creature" with the promise "they shall recover." "The Lord shall raise them up."

The Brazen Serpent—A Type of Christ

God ratified His Word to the dying Israelites by sending them the added Word, "everyone that is bitten, when he looketh upon it (the brazen serpent, the type of Calvary) shall live." If bodily healing is not provided in the Atonement, why were these dying Israelites required to look at the type of the Atonement for bodily healing? As their curse was removed by the lifting up of the type of Christ, so ours is removed by the lifting up of Christ, the Antitype. Since the Spirit is given to us to make Christ a reality, why should we not look to Christ Himself with as much expectation as they did to the type?

It will be well to note that they could not look at the brass snake and their symptoms at the same time. Abraham's faith waxed strong while he looked to the promise of God. Some people reverse this. Their faith waxes weak while they look at their symptoms and forget the promises. God's Word is the only solid basis for our faith. God healed by sending His Word. We will miss healing if we allow our symptoms to hinder us from expecting what His Word promises.

The Second Step

The second step toward being healed is to be sure you are right with God. Our redemptive blessings are conditional. After we hear the Gospel, and know what it offers, Jesus says, "Repent ye and believe the gospel." Only those who are right with God can follow these instructions. When seeking healing for our bodies, there should be no compromise with the adversary of our souls, because it is he who is the author of our diseases. Jesus has promised to destroy the works of the devil in our bodies. He cannot legally do that while we are clinging to the work of the devil in our souls. It is hard to exercise faith for the removal of one part of the devil's work while we allow a worse part to remain. Until a man squarely faces and settles the question of obedience to God, he is not on believing ground. James says, "Confess your faults one to another . . . that ye may be healed." It is God's will "that thou mayest prosper and be in health even as thy soul prospereth." "If I regard iniquity in my heart the Lord will not hear me." It is when our hearts do not condemn us that we have confidence toward God.

The command for the sick to "send for the elders" was first written to Christians who had been *filled with the Spirit.* There is something wrong when a man desires the blessing but not the Blesser; His mercy but not *Himself.* It is not proper to seek His mercy while rejecting His will. Do not ask for a little blessing while rejecting a big one. It is impossible to receive and reject divine blessings at the same time. God is waiting to say to Satan and disease what He said to Pharaoh, "Let my people go, that they may *serve* me" (Exodus 7:16). "Our first consideration, in all things, even in asking for the restoration of bodily health, should be the glory of God" (Rev. P. Gavin Duffy).

Strength for service to God is the only proper basis of approach when seeking health at His hand. The anointing with oil for healing is a symbol and sign of consecration. We must desire our health for God's glory.

> What then does the anointing mean? Turn to Leviticus 8:10–12, and you get God's answer to the question. "And Moses took the anointing oil, and anointed the tabernacle and *all* that was therein, and sanctified them," that is, he *set them apart for God*. The anointing "with oil in the name of the Lord," was an act of dedication and consecration, implying on the part of one anointed, a full surrender to God of his hands to work for Him and for Him alone, of his feet to walk for Him and Him alone, his eyes to see, his lips to speak, his ears to hear for Him and Him alone, and his whole body to be the temple of the Holy Spirit.
>
> Rev. R. A. Torrey

"Beloved, I wish above all things that thou mayest prosper and be in health, *even as thy soul prospereth*" (3 John 2).

The Holy Spirit tells us to submit ourselves to God before He says "resist the devil," because no one can successfully resist the devil until he submits himself to God. When the devil is *thus* resisted, he will not merely walk away, but he will literally run or "*flee from you*" (James 4:7)!

The curse, including the different diseases catalogued in Deuteronomy 28, came on the people because their obedience and their service was not "with gladness and joyfulness of heart." The condition of heart that was responsible for the coming of those diseases mentioned in that chapter is not the right condition for their removal. In other words, the condition of heart that was responsible for the curse in that day is not the condition of heart in which to come to Him for the removal of the curse in our day.

God's Promises Are Only to the Obedient

It is to those who will delight themselves in the Lord that He gives the desires of their heart (Psalm 37:4). God has not lowered the standard for the Day of Grace. It is only to the obedient, those who will "diligently hearken to the voice of the LORD" and "do that which is right in his sight," that it is said, "The LORD will take away from *thee* all sickness" (Exodus 15:26; Deuteronomy 7:15).

"Faith, you see, is the union of our hearts and wills with God's will and purpose; and where this unity is lacking, results are impossible. This is a *very important spiritual law* to which, in our times, we have been woefully blind" (Rev. P. Gavin Duffy). God says, of fearing the Lord and departing from evil, "*It* shall [itself] be health [Hebrew, *medicine*] to thy navel, and marrow [Hebrew, *moistening*] to thy bones" (Proverbs 3:7–8).

Faith always implies obedience. Paul instructed the Ephesians to obey the fifth commandment, "that it may be well with thee, and thou mayest live long on the earth" (Ephesians 6:3). Naaman's surrender and obedience to the Word of God was complete before he was healed.

It is to those who "walk uprightly" that it is said, "No good thing will he withhold" (Psalm 84:11). Therefore, before seeking anything from God, we should yield ourselves to the "first and great commandment." "Thou shalt love the LORD thy God with all thy heart." God says, "*Because* he hath set his love upon me, *therefore* will I deliver him" (Psalm 91:14). He "keepeth covenant and mercy with *them that love him* and keep his commandments to a thousand generations" (Deuteronomy 7:9). *Therefore*, like the leper, let us come and worship Him when asking for healing.

"Length of days is in her [Wisdom's] right hand; and in her left hand riches and honour" (Proverbs 3:16). Marry her (Wisdom) and you get her possessions. Wisdom is here represented as a bountiful Queen, reaching forth blessings with both hands to all who will become subject to her government.

It is for "them whose heart is perfect toward him" that "the eyes of the LORD run to and fro throughout the whole earth, to shew himself strong" (2 Chronicles 16:9).

"A sound heart is the *life of the flesh*: but envy the rottenness of the bones" (Proverbs 14:30). An unsound heart is worse than an unsound stomach. A diseased soul is worse than a diseased body. A disordered will is worse than a disordered liver. Paul said, "the body . . . for the Lord" before he said, "the Lord for the body."

The Bible teaches that the body is "bought with a price: therefore glorify God in your body, and in your spirit, *which are God's*" (1 Corinthians 6:20). "I beseech you therefore, brethren, by the *mercies* of God, that ye present your bodies a living sacrifice, . . . which is your reasonable service" (Romans 12:1). Therefore present your body to Him if you want it healed. It is not until after it becomes His property that He promises to repair it.

First to the Cross for Cleansing

"The sure way for the sick is, first to the cross for cleansing, then to the upper room for the gift of the Spirit, then to the mount appointed for a life commission, and, lastly, to the Great Physician for strength for service" (Bryant). "If the Spirit of him that raised up Jesus from the dead dwell in you, he that raised up Christ from the dead shall also quicken your mortal bodies by his Spirit that dwelleth *in* you" (Romans 8:11). In Christ, the true Vine, there is all the life for our souls and bodies that we need. How are we to possess and enjoy this except by our *union* with the Vine. It is not apart from Him, but "*in Him*" that "ye are complete" (Colossians 2:10).

Substitution without union is not sufficient for our possession and enjoyment of the life of the Vine. If you need a miracle, get in tune with the Miracle-Worker. We enjoy the Life of the Vine by our perfect union with the Vine. Asking for healing while refusing to be led by the Spirit is like asking a carpenter to repair the house while refusing to let him into the house.

"As many as touched [Him] were made perfectly whole" (Matthew 14:36). You cannot touch Him with a reservation. Like the woman who pressed through the throng and touched Him, you must "elbow" selfishness, disobedience, unconfessed sins, lukewarmness, public opinion, traditions of men and articles written against divine healing out of your way. In fact you must often press beyond your own pastor, who may be unenlightened in this part of the Gospel. Press beyond doubts, double-mindedness, symptoms, feelings and the lying Serpent.

The Holy Spirit, who is sent to execute for us the blessings of redemption, is our Paraclete or Helper. He is ready to help us press through and beyond all of these obstacles to the place where we can touch Him for our needs. God is waiting to pour out the Holy Spirit in fullness upon us. He comes as Christ's executive to execute for us all the blessings provided by Calvary. These blessings are pledged to us in His seven redemptive and covenant names.

It is still true that as many as touch Him are made whole. How do we touch Him? By believing His promise. This is an infallible way of touching Christ for anything He has promised. We touch Him by asking and believing that He hears our prayers when we pray. When the woman touched Him, it was her faith that made her whole. This was not a mere physical touch, for "it is the Spirit that quickeneth [gives life]; the flesh profiteth nothing." Millions of sinners have thus touched Him for the yet greater miracle of the new birth.

Not Mere Contact, but Union

As the sick touched Him and were made whole when Christ walked on the earth, so now it is the privilege of all to actually touch Him. The touch now unites us to Christ in a closer union than it did then. This is not mere contact, but union as real as the branch and the vine. All that is in the Vine, including both spiritual and physical life, belongs to us, the branches.

The touch, by faith, can now bring us under the full control of the Holy Spirit as it could not do during Christ's earthly ministry, for "the Holy Ghost was not yet given." He is the Miracle-Worker. Jesus is not less a Savior and Healer since being glorified—He is *greater*. The privilege of touching Him now is much greater than when He was here in person, because more can now be received by the touch. From God's right hand He has more to give. He said, "It is expedient [profitable] for you that I go away." He went away to send the Spirit. Since the Spirit comes to reveal Christ as He could not be revealed before He went away, why cannot we approach Him for healing with at least as much faith as those who thronged Him in that day?

The foregoing shows the great importance of being right with God before asking for healing. The blessing of being right with God is a thousand times more desirable and enjoyable than the healing itself. I have seen the afflicted in body radiantly happy; but sinners in perfect health have been so unhappy as to commit suicide.

The Third Step

We will now endeavor to make plain how to *appropriate* healing. Getting things from God is like playing checkers. After one person moves, he has nothing to do until the other player moves. Each man moves in his own turn. So, when God has provided healing, or any other blessing, and sent us His Word, it is our move before He will move again. Our move is to expect what He promises *when* we pray. This will cause us to *act* our faith before we *see* the healing. The healing comes in the next move, which is God's move.

God never moves out of His turn, but He always moves when it is His turn. When Noah was "warned of God *of things not seen as yet*," his move was to *believe* that the flood was coming. He *acted on his faith* by building the ship on dry land. So, when God says to "any sick . . . the prayer of faith shall save the sick, and the Lord shall raise him up," you, like Noah, are informed by God "of things not seen as yet." Your move is the same as Noah's, which is to believe and act accordingly. Fallen nature is governed by what it sees, by its senses. Faith is governed by the pure Word of God, and is nothing less than *expecting* God to do what He promises. It is treating Him like an honest being.

By *expectation* I do not mean hope. One writer has well said, "We hope for what *may* be possible, but we expect what *must* be possible . . . with that expectancy that shuts out doubt or fear of failure, and shows unshakable confidence."

Faith never waits to *see* before it believes. It "cometh by *hearing*" about "things not seen as yet." It "is the evidence of things not seen." All that a man of faith needs is to know that God has spoken. This imparts perfect certainty to the soul. "Thus saith the Lord" settles everything. "It is written" is all that faith needs.

Faith always blows the ram's horn *before*, not after, the walls are down. Faith never judges according to the sight of the eyes. It is the evidence of things not seen but promised. Faith rests on far more solid ground than the evidence of the senses. It is the Word of God, which "abideth forever." Our senses may deceive us, but God's Word never!

When the little girl is promised a new dress next Saturday, faith is the actual expectation that she has and manifests between now and Saturday. When Saturday comes and she sees the new dress, faith for the new dress stops. Real faith always has corresponding actions. The little girl, because of her faith, claps her hands and says, "Goody! Goody! I am going to have a new dress next Saturday!" She runs to tell her playmates that she has the answer to her request.

God Cannot Lie

Jesus, at the grave of Lazarus, looked up, and said, "I thank Thee, Father, that Thou *hast* heard me." Lazarus was still dead. The little girl is not afraid to testify in advance that she is to have a new dress. When her playmates say, "How do you know you are?" she confidently replies, "Mama promised it!" Now, you have a better reason for expecting healing than the little girl has for expecting a new dress because the mother may die before Saturday, but God cannot. The mother can lie, but God cannot. The house may burn down with the mother's money. Every case of faith in history was a well-grounded assurance produced by the promise of God alone. It was acted upon before there was anything visible to encourage the assurance, as with the little girl "between now and Saturday."

Faith looks "not at the things that are seen." There was no flood in sight when Noah built his ark. Stone walls had never before fallen down at the blowing of rams' horns and shouting. They were merely expecting what God promised. When they acted on their faith by blowing the rams' horns while the walls were still up, this was *their* move. Then, of course, *God* moved in His turn, and down came the walls!

The whole eleventh chapter of Hebrews is written to show how each one who had faith acted "between now and Saturday." God is so well pleased with the actings of faith that He has listed in detail many cases in the eleventh chapter of Hebrews. "By faith, Noah" acted so-and-so. "By faith Jacob" acted so-and-so. "By faith Moses" acted so-and-so. "By faith the walls of Jericho fell down." "By faith Abraham" acted so-and-so when everything seemed contrary to what God had promised. It was by considering the *promise of God* (not her barrenness) that Sarah received strength to become a mother when she was past age. These all acted with *nothing but the Word of God as their reason for expecting the thing He had promised.*

It is the same with every case of faith in history. Jonah's symptoms were very real when he was inside the fish, and he did not deny them; but he called them "lying vanities." In other words, any symptoms that make us doubt the fact that God is "plenteous in mercy to *all*" that call upon Him, should be regarded as "lying vanities." Jonah said, "They that observe lying vanities forsake their own mercy." Instead of listening to Satan and watching our symptoms, we must be "workers together" with God who heals by *sending His Word* and keeping it!

We must cooperate with Him by being occupied, not with what the devil says, but with *the Word He sends for our healing.*

Symptoms May Linger

Even when we do act our faith, symptoms do not always disappear instantly. After Hezekiah was healed, it was three days before he was strong enough to go up to the House of the Lord. In John 4:50–52 the nobleman "believed the word that Jesus had spoken unto him." When he met his servants he enquired of them the hour when his dying son "began to amend."

The Bible differentiates between the "gifts of healing" and the gift of "miracles." Christ could do no *miracle* in Nazareth because of their unbelief, but He healed a few sick ones. If everyone were to be made perfectly whole instantly, there would be no place for the gifts of healing. It would be all miracles. Many people miss healing by trying to confine God to miracles. Christ's promise is that "they shall recover," but He does not say "instantly."

The symptoms of life in a tree remain for a time after the tree is cut down.

"Faith means that we are confident of what we hope for, convinced of what we do not see" (Hebrews 11:1 Moffatt's translation). We are convinced because God, who cannot lie, has spoken. *How all-sufficient is this reason for believing!* Faith is most rational. It is not, as many unthinking persons suppose, believing without evidence. It is believing because of the very highest possible evidence, God's Word, which is "settled in heaven." The apostle James says, "I will show you by my deeds what faith is" (James 2:18 Moffatt's translation). Faith is being so convinced of the absolute truth of the declarations of God, which are recorded in the Bible, that we act on them.

Faith Both Rational and Safe

What can be more rational and what can be more safe and certain than faith?

Faith is to receive the written promise of God as His direct message to us. His promise means the same as if He appeared and said to us, "I have heard your prayer." The Word of God is made life to our bodies in exactly the same way that it is made life to our souls, by believing His promise.

I have known some who had prayed for healing for as long as forty years without receiving it. As soon as they were told how to appropriate the healing, it has come sometimes in a moment. We do not have to pray for forty years or for one week for the blessing that Christ is eager to bestow. His compassionate heart yearns to heal us more than we have the capacity to desire it. We keep Him waiting until we have the "faith that cometh by hearing" and act on that faith. God will not cheat and move out of His turn.

We see Jesus bore our diseases as well as our sins on the cross and therefore we need not bear them. Our next step is to appropriate by faith. This is the only scriptural way. God gave us this part of our inheritance nearly two thousand years ago and *He* is the waiting One. He is waiting for us to appropriate the blessing by faith. Two thousand years ago God "put away sin." Two thousand years ago "God laid on Christ the iniquity of us all." Two thousand years ago Christ "Himself took our infirmities, and bare our sicknesses." God is the waiting party. He is waiting for us to be shown how to appropriate the blessing He has *already* given. Second Peter 3:9 says, "The Lord is not slack [slow] concerning his promise . . . but is longsuffering to us-ward." Or, as Weymouth translates, "The Lord is not slow in fulfilling His promise, . . . But He bears patiently with you." He is not slow concerning His promises, but *we* are *slow* and *He is patient* with us.

Most of us could have been saved five years earlier than we were. God was not making us wait, but we were making Him wait. It is the same with our healing.

When Ye Pray, Not Afterward

Now, in Mark 11:24, Jesus tells us exactly how to appropriate any of the blessings purchased for us by His death. Having promised all that we need, He says, "What things soever ye desire, *when ye pray.*" This does not mean after you pray for twenty years. It is not after you get well, but while you are sick. "*When ye pray,* believe that ye receive them, and ye *shall* have them." The condition of receiving what we ask from God is to believe that He answers our prayers when we pray and that we "shall recover" according to His promise.

When you pray for healing, Christ authorizes you to consider your prayer answered. It is the same as when He stood at the grave of Lazarus and said, "I thank thee, Father, that thou *hast* heard me," before He saw Lazarus come forth from the grave. When we ask for healing, Christ bids us say, with faith, "I thank Thee, Father, that Thou *hast* heard me," before we have yet seen the answer to our prayer.

Faith is when God's Word alone is our reason for believing that our prayer is answered, before we see or feel.

> Jesus declared, "The *Words* that I speak unto you *they* are Spirit and they are life." John says, "The Word was God." To receive the written Words of Christ as the direct message to us is faith. This is the way the Word of God becomes life to us, both in our healing and in our salvation. For instance, the act of believing and receiving Christ according to John 1:12 is synonymous with the act of God, which gives us, by His power, the new birth. By this same process also is divine healing imparted to our bodies.
>
> Author not known

Another has said, concerning the woman who touched Jesus' garment, that faith, fact and feeling is the order of healing that God never departs from. If *we* depart from this order neither faith, fact nor feeling will be as we desire because they will not be as God desires.

First Thessalonians 2:13 says it is "the word of God which effectually worketh also in you that believe." When His Word convinces us that our prayer is answered, before we have yet seen the answer, the Word begins to effectually work in us.

> God's Word never fails to work in those who accept it as such, because they are not entertaining doubts as to it being fulfilled in their own experiences. . . . God has given all His blessings to Faith, He has none left to bestow upon unbelief.
>
> Harriet S. Bainbridge

When people say to me, "I do not know that it is God's will to heal me," I ask them, "Is it God's will to keep His promise?" It is not, Have I faith enough? but, Is God honest? It is not a question of how we feel, but what the facts are. Should the little girl get sick the next day, and feel badly, it has nothing to do with her mother buying her the new dress on Saturday. The Scriptures say, "If we ask anything according to his will he heareth us." Is this true or not?

Does God answer prayer? If you will steadfastly "believe that ye receive" (Mark 11:24) the answer to your prayer, and act on your faith, every one of you will be healed, though not always instantly.

God always moves after our move. This is the acting out of a "full assurance" produced alone by His promise before we see the answer to our prayer. Since healing is by faith, and "faith without works is dead," it is when we begin to *act* on our faith that God begins to heal.

Our Faith Makes God Act

Our "work of faith" sets God to working. We cannot all act in the same way. As the ten lepers went, they were healed. Jonah when inside the fish could not "went," but he did act on his faith by saying, while still in the fish, "I will sacrifice with the voice of thanksgiving." Acting on our faith by praising and thanking God in advance has been, throughout history, His appointed way for our appropriation of all His blessings. Hebrews 13:15 teaches us that our thank offering, our "sacrifice of praise," is to be offered in advance for the blessing God has promised. It is only then that we can expect an answer. Psalm 50:14–15 says, "Offer unto God thanksgiving; and pay thy vows unto the most High: and call upon me in the day of trouble: I will deliver thee, and thou shalt glorify me."

Here, as elsewhere, we are required, as Jonah did, to offer thanksgiving while we are still in trouble. Perhaps this was the very promise he claimed. "Let the . . . needy praise thy name." Praise God in advance while you are still in need. "Let us come before his presence with thanksgiving" does not mean to get healed and then go from His presence thanking Him. It means to come to Him with thanksgiving for healing before being healed. "*Enter* into his gates with thanksgiving and into his courts with praise." We should go away with thanksgiving, but this is not faith.

Faith is what we have before we are healed. "They shall praise the Lord that *seek* him." "Thou shalt call thy walls salvation, and thy gates praise." Without praise we are up against a solid wall with no gate; but when we begin praising and appropriating, we hang our own gate and walk through. "Be glad and rejoice; for the Lord *will* do great things." Accordingly, "they were continually in the Temple praising and blessing God." This was not after, but before, they were filled with the Holy Spirit. It was "when they lifted up their voice and praised the Lord" that "the glory of the Lord filled the House of God." "They believed his *words* [not their symptoms, not the "father of lies"] and sang his praises."

Make Satan Listen to Your Praises

Instead of your listening to the "father of lies," make *him* listen to your praising God for His promise! "Let everything that hath breath praise the Lord." The sick man has breath. In other words, while you are still sick, praise Him because you are going to recover according to His promise. "Let not your heart be troubled." "Be careful [distracted] for nothing; but . . . with thanksgiving let your requests be made known unto God." "Casting all your care upon him; for he careth for you."

Every sick Christian, while sick, has a thousand times more to be happy over than the most cheerful sinner in perfect health.

Praise God, because "faith without works is dead." "In everything give thanks, for this is the will of God concerning you." "I will bless the Lord at *all* times, his praise shall continually be in my mouth." Since everything that hath breath is commanded to praise the Lord, the only scriptural excuse for not praising Him is to be out of breath. "By Him, therefore, let us offer the sacrifice of praise to God continually, . . . the fruit of our lips giving thanks to his name." "Whoso offereth praise glorifieth me." "Because Thy loving kindness *is better than life*, my lips shall praise thee." Praise Him "because it is a good thing to give thanks unto the Lord." "Give thanks at the remembrance of his holiness." Praise Him because to withhold praise will show either unbelief or ingratitude. Praise Him because "praise is comely for the upright." Praise Him because God inhabits the praises of His people. Paul and Silas sang praises at midnight with their backs bleeding and their feet in the stocks, and God sang bass with an earthquake, which set them free.

Real faith rejoices in the promise of God as *if* it saw the deliverance, and was enjoying it.

With three great armies against Jehoshaphat, which humanly speaking would mean annihilation, they praised the Lord "with a loud voice on high." The only evidence that their prayer was answered was the naked Word of God; and *that* only through human lips. The next day, when they went out to the battle, and began to sing and praise, the Lord in His turn moved and set ambushments against the enemy and the victory was won (2 Chronicles 20:21–22). "We have also a more sure word of prophecy"; for "holy men of God spake as they were moved by the Holy Ghost" (2 Peter 1:19, 21).

As in Eden the enemy succeeded in making void God's testimony as to the results of eating the forbidden fruit, so now he seeks to make void God's testimony as to the results of believing the Gospel. After God said, "In the day thou eatest thereof thou shalt surely die," the serpent said, "Thou shalt not surely die," and now, when God's Word plainly says, "They shall lay hands on the sick and they *shall* recover," the same serpent seeks to persuade them that they shall *not* recover. Is it rational to believe the "father of lies" in preference to the Son of God, who is Incarnate Truth? When coming to God for salvation or healing, it is essential for each one to decide whether he shall allow the hiss of the serpent to rise above the voice of God.

> Blessed are the ears that hear the pulses of the Divine whisper, and give no heed to the many whisperings of the world.
>
> Thomas à Kempis

When, after you have been anointed for healing, Satan tells you that you will not recover, like Jesus, say to him,

"It is written:" "They *shall* recover." "The Lord *shall* raise him up" (James 5:15). In this same passage, "in the name of the Lord" means the same as if the Lord Himself anointed you. Expect Him to honor His own ordinance and His own promise.

Why Listen to the Devil?

All the devil heard from the lips of Christ when tempting Him was, "It is written!" "It is written!" "It is written!" (Matthew 4:4, 7, 10). "Then the devil leaveth him" (Matthew 4:11). But all we hear from some people is, "The devil says!" "The devil says!" "The devil says!" as though Christ's Words were of less consequence than those of the devil! This was Christ's way. It is the most successful way of resisting the devil. Let us not try another! "Neither give place to the devil" (Ephesians 4:27). "Resist the devil, and he will flee from you" (James 4:7). There is just one way of resisting the devil; and that is by steadfastly believing and acting upon God's Word.

Whenever we are affected by any voice more than the voice of God, we have forsaken the Lord's way for our healing.

What reason have you for doubting? You have no more reason for doubting than the sinner has when he repents and asks forgiveness of his sins. You have exactly the same reason for expecting to be healed that you had for expecting to be saved. "You have His Word for it, and if you cannot accept that to the point of acting upon it, then your faith is still very far from what it should be" (Duffy).

The Lord's Compassion—A Basis for Faith

What a basis for faith is the Lord's compassion! Since Christ has redeemed us from sickness, surely His love and faithfulness may be trusted. The cross is a sure foundation and a perfect reason for the exercise of faith.

Let us put our sickness away by faith, as we would put away sin. The consecrated Christian will not consciously tolerate sin for a moment, and yet how tolerant some are toward sickness. They will even pet and indulge their aches and pains instead of resisting them as the words of the devil.

Harriet S. Bainbridge says that the Lord Jesus has declared, concerning the sin, sorrow, and physical misery of Adam's race, "It is finished." He has offered unto each one of us the gift of the Holy Spirit to enable us to realize and enjoy the great salvation He purchased for us. To believe without doubt that Christ's Words, "It is finished," are a literal statement of an unchangeable fact invariably brings deliverance. The serpent is still denying this great saying of Christ to our great loss, just as he caused Eve to forget and disregard words that God had plainly spoken to *her*. Our redemption from sickness was actually accomplished in the body of our crucified Lord. It is by wholeheartedly believing and receiving what God declares in His written Word about the matter that the Holy Spirit gives us the personal experience of Christ as our physician.

Present-day Results of Believing God

Following these instructions has brought soundness to thousands who had before been taught that the age of miracles was past. They had been told that God wanted people to remain sick for His glory, etc., etc. Those born blind are now seeing. Deaf and dumb mutes from birth are now hearing and speaking. Cripples from birth are now perfectly whole. Epileptics for years are now free and rejoicing. Many who were dying with cancers are now well and praying the prayer of faith for the healing of others. God is no respecter of persons. "If man will purge himself from these he shall be a vessel unto honor, sanctified, and meet for the Master's use, and thoroughly prepared unto every good work." This is never true while we are sick in bed. God's New Covenant provides that we each "shall be made perfect in every good work to do his will." This cannot be while we are sick. This shows His willingness to make us well. In fact, He is eager.

He cannot keep His Covenant with us without taking away our sicknesses and fulfilling the number of our days, according to His promise.

Since it is "by his stripes we are healed," let us not forget what our healing cost. With gratitude and love, and consecrated service to God, let us stand on His promise and "blow the ram's horn" of faith and thanksgiving until the walls of our affliction fall down flat.

Faith does not wait for the walls to fall down; faith shouts them down!

6

Appropriating Faith

The apostle Paul in his letter to the Galatians tells us exactly how God works miracles. "He [God] therefore that ministereth to you the Spirit [the Spirit is the Miracle-Worker], and worketh miracles among you, doeth he it by the works of the law, or by the hearing [message] of faith? Even as Abraham believed God" (Galatians 3:5–6).

Moffatt translates this passage: "When He supplies you with the Spirit and works miracles among you, is it because you do what the Law commands or because you believe the gospel message? Why, it is as with Abraham, he had faith."

In this passage God tells us that He works miracles upon our bodies in exactly the same way as upon our souls. It is by having us hear and "believe the Gospel message." In fact God's way of doing everything is by making promises and then by fulfilling them wherever they produce faith. He says it is with us as with Abraham. How was it with Abraham? Note carefully:

- He simply believed the Word of God. "He had faith" that God would do exactly as He promised.

116

- He was "fully persuaded" by the Word of God alone.
- He held fast the beginning of his confidence when his faith was tested.
- He was wholly occupied with the Word of God in the matter.
- He refused to cast away his confidence when God, by telling him to offer Isaac, was apparently removing the visible encouragement to his faith.

He "considered not his own body" or the fact that he was about a hundred years old. He didn't look at "the deadness of Sarah's womb" (Romans 4:19) as any barrier or any reason for doubting that Isaac would be born. These things, which, according to nature, made the birth of Isaac impossible, were not considered by Abraham as the slightest reason for doubting. He knew his age; he recognized the barrenness of Sarah. He weighed the difficulties; but notwithstanding the impossible, he believed God.

Under utterly hopeless circumstances, by "looking unto the promise of God" he "waxed strong in faith," being "fully persuaded" ("absolutely certain," Weymouth) that God would fulfill His promise. Note well: It was by "looking unto the promise of God" that Abraham "waxed strong in faith." "Every one that . . . looketh upon it" [the brazen serpent, God's remedy and God's promise] was likewise the condition God required for the healing of the dying Israelites (Numbers 21:8). When coming to God for healing, be sure that this shall be your attitude, because there is no healing promised except on this condition.

The Basis of Our Faith

When we base faith on our improvement, or are affected by our symptoms or by what we see or feel instead of by the

Word of God alone, just to that extent ours is not real faith. To be occupied with what we see or feel is to exactly reverse the condition God lays down for us to follow. "Every one that . . . looketh upon it, shall live." This simply means that every one who, like Abraham, occupies himself with God's promise so that he is no longer affected by symptoms "shall recover." It means, the Word of God (not what we see or feel) shall be the basis of our faith. Our looking unto the promise of God is a good reason for looking to God for mercy. Then there is no time to stop looking until God withdraws His Word.

Note that it was by *continuing* to look unto the promise of God that Abraham experienced the miracle. To be occupied and influenced by symptoms instead of God's Word is to question the veracity of God. Instead of making God a liar, Jonah, from within the fish, gave the name "lying vanities" to the symptoms and circumstances that seemed to stand in the way of his expecting God's mercy. Realizing that it was *symptoms* and not God that was lying to him, he said, "They that observe *lying vanities* forsake their own mercy." God never refuses to give mercy, but many "forsake" it by observing their symptoms. The symptoms are real, but become "lying vanities" when they say to us that God is not plenteous in mercy to all that call on Him.

Abraham's faith was not based on anything he saw. You must see to it that yours is not. All that Abraham could see was contrary to what he was expecting. After Isaac was born, Abraham had a prop for his faith. Through Isaac, "all the nations of the earth shall be blessed." With his eyes upon Isaac, the channel through which God was to fulfill the rest of His promise, it was easy to believe. So God tested his faith, by telling him to offer Isaac, to destroy the channel. This did not daunt Abraham. Real faith thrives on a test. Since he still had God's Word for it, he was ready to remove every visible encouragement to his expectation and yet continue to be "fully persuaded." God had to halt him or he would have offered Isaac. This test was God's way of perfecting his faith, not of destroying it.

If, after coming to God for healing, He finds you more encouraged by your improvement than by His Word, He may find it necessary to test your faith. This is to teach you the glorious lesson of believing His Word, when every sense contradicts Him. *Faith has to do only with the Word of God.*

In Hebrews 10:35–36 God says to all whose faith is based on His Word, "Cast not away therefore your confidence, which hath great recompence of reward. For ye have need of patience, that, after ye have done the will of God, ye might receive the promise." "For we are made partakers of Christ, if we hold the beginning of our confidence stedfast unto the end" (Hebrews 3:14).

Many act directly contrary to this. After being anointed and prayed for, instead of rejoicing in the promise of God, I have heard some say in disappointment, "I thought sure I was going to be healed." I knew instantly that they had never caught the idea of what faith is. Their idea was to get well first, and then to believe that God had heard prayer. If God's Word were the sole reason for their expectation, they would have held fast the beginning of their confidence. It is never proper or reasonable to cast away your confidence as long as you have the Word of God as its basis. It is promised that we shall be partakers only on the condition that we "hold the beginning of our confidence stedfast." During the interim between God's promise and its fulfillment, instead of watching symptoms and casting away his confidence because he had nothing visible to encourage him, Abraham did exactly the reverse. By "looking unto the *promise* of God, he wavered not through unbelief; but waxed strong through faith, giving glory to God" (Romans 4:20 ASV). After Jonah prayed for mercy from within the fish, he did not cast away his confidence because there was no visible proof that his prayer was heard. He held fast his confidence and added to it, in advance, "the sacrifice of thanksgiving." After marching around the walls of Jericho, Joshua and the children of Israel did not cast away their confidence because the walls of the city were still up. Their faith was based on God's Word: "I have given unto thine hand Jericho." If none of these cast away their confidence, why should you?

Your state of mind should be the same as Noah's when he was building a ship on dry land and putting pitch into the cracks to keep the water out. In his mind, the fact of a coming flood was fully settled, and the Word of God was the sole reason for this state of mind. Your state of mind should be the same as Abraham's. With him, the matter of Isaac being born was fully settled, even though all the symptoms were to the contrary. God's Word to you concerning your healing is just as clear and explicit as it was to Abraham.

In Mark 11:24 Jesus tells us exactly the conditions He requires for our appropriation of any of the blessings He has promised. He says, "What things soever ye desire, when ye pray, believe that ye receive them, and ye shall have them." That is, "Ye shall have them" *after* you believe He has heard your prayer. As Jesus said, "I thank thee that thou *hast* heard me," while Lazarus was still dead, we should be able to say, "I thank Thee that Thou hast heard me" while we are still sick. "Ye shall have them" is your answer from Jesus and is also your proof that your prayer has been heard. To faith, the *Word* of God is the *voice* of God. He has not promised us that our healing shall begin until *after* we believe that He has heard our prayer. "If we ask anything according to His will, He heareth us." If this is true, then believe your prayer has been heard when you really pray. We must be able to say, "We know we have the petition we desire of Him," not because we see the answer, but because "God is faithful who also will do it."

It is never proper to base faith on our improvement after prayer. I have heard some say, with great delight, "Oh, I am so much better since I was prayed for; now I know I will get well." This means that in the place of God's promise they have some other reason for expecting to get well. *There is no reason for faith as good as the Word of God.* Suppose, as soon as I pray for a man's healing, he could know he was just 50 percent improved. This improvement in his condition is not near as good a reason for knowing he will entirely recover as is the promise of God. The promise of God is a better reason even though after prayer he should become 50 percent worse. Suppose you promise your child a certain thing and the next day you find that she is expecting exactly what you promised, but not because you promised it. She has some other reason for expecting it. This would grieve you. It would prove she did not trust your word.

It honors God to believe Him even while every sense contradicts Him. He promises to honor those who honor Him. God has promised to respond only to the faith that is produced by and rests in His Word, His promise. Some expect to believe they have been heard as soon as they feel better. He did not say that He sent *better feelings* to produce faith and then healed them. "He sent his *word*, and healed them." God Himself "*sent his word.*" We did not "*worm*" it out of Him. How absurd, then, to doubt it. Is it not more rational to expect God to keep His promise than to expect Him to break it? Really, nothing can be more ridiculous or absurd than to allow symptoms or feelings to cause us to doubt the fulfillment of God's promises. Suppose your child, after being promised a new dress, should sprain her ankle and should cast away her confidence for the dress because the ankle was painful. You say to her, "My dear child, I promised to get you the new dress. Can you not believe my word?" She answers: "But, Mother, my ankle still hurts; it doesn't feel a bit better; it seems to be getting worse." How absurd is such reasoning. Now if it be absurd to doubt one promise because of pain, then it is equally ridiculous to doubt any promise. Suppose again, that after you promise her the new dress, she runs to the mirror to see if she looks any more "dressed up." She then says: "I cannot see any difference; I do not look a bit better"; and then gives up the idea of having a new dress.

To learn how to believe that God hears us when we pray is a much greater blessing than is the healing itself. Then the prayer of faith can be repeated ten thousand times, for ourselves and others. In this way our whole life can be spent in obtaining the fulfillment of divine promises.

We have seen how Abraham experienced a miracle; and God says it is with us "as with Abraham." In this same way, we may all receive the fulfillment of God's promises, *"who also* walk in *the steps of that faith of our father Abraham"* (Romans 4:12).

7

How to Receive Healing from Christ

Numbers 21 records an instance of God's judgment. The Israelites had been bitten by fiery serpents and were dying. God had instructed that a brazen serpent be lifted up on a pole. This was a type of the Atonement that Christ adopted and applied to Himself. The condition to be met for healing is given in verse 8: "It shall come to pass, that every one that is bitten, *when he looketh upon it*, shall live."

If, as some teach, healing is not provided by Christ's Atonement, then why were these dying Israelites required to look at the type of the *Atonement* for bodily healing? Since both forgiveness and healing came to them all by an expectant look at the type of Calvary, why cannot we all receive as much from Christ, the Antitype? If we cannot, then the type is placed on higher ground than Christ Himself, and the type becomes a false prophecy.

"Every One That Looketh"

Notice that none were to receive healing except on this condition: "Every one that *LOOKETH*."

LOOKING means to be *occupied and influenced* with what we are looking at. It is the equivalent of Abraham's refusing to consider his own body. He waxed strong in faith by looking unto the promises of God. Being occupied and influenced by our feelings or symptoms is reversing the conditions that God requires.

LOOKING means *attention*. God gave the covenant of healing and revealed Himself as our healer by the redemptive name Jehovah-Rapha. The condition He laid down was that they should "*hearken diligently . . . and do all His commandments.*" This means *attention and heed* to His Word. In Mark 4:24 Jesus also taught us that it is by our attention and heed to God's Word that we measure His blessings to ourselves. "The Word of God is the seed." Like all seed, when it is put into good ground, it has the power to do its own work. Attention and heed to the Word of God is the way to get it into "good ground" and to keep it there.

Satan cannot hinder the "seed" from doing its work unless we allow him to get the seed out of the ground. He can only do this by getting you to turn your attention away from the Word of God to your symptoms. Jonah called his symptoms "lying vanities" and said, while still in the great fish, "I will *LOOK* again toward thy holy temple." Then, we hear him offering "the sacrifice of thanksgiving." This shows what *LOOKING* means.

LOOKING also means *expectation*. To look unto God for salvation means to *expect* salvation from Him. He says to us all: "*Look* unto Me, all ye ends of the earth, and be ye saved." Since God has provided and promised healing, we should dismiss from our minds the slightest thought of failing to be healed.

The word *LOOKETH* is also translated "consider." We read that Sarah *"considered* that she could rely upon Him who had promised." Instead of considering her age, she received faith by considering the Word of God.

The word *LOOKETH* is in the continuous present tense. It is not a mere *glance,* but a continuous "stare" until you are well. It was a *"stedfast* faith" that brought the fulfillment of God's promise to Abraham. The healing process goes on while we are *looking* unto the promise. We are to think faith, speak faith, act faith and keep it until the promise is fulfilled. By being occupied with symptoms or feelings, we violate the conditions and thereby turn off the switch to His power.

The Sight of Faith

We read in Hebrews 11:23–27 that Moses "endured, as [by] *seeing him who is invisible."* As far as the optic nerve is concerned, "faith is the evidence of things *not seen."* But as far as the enlightened "eyes of our understanding" are concerned, faith *is* the evidence *of things seen.* Walking by *faith* is walking by *sight* of a better kind. We are to spend our lives *looking* at far better things than can be seen with the optic nerve. We see with the eye of faith the glorious things that are invisible to the natural eye. After all, it is the mind and not the optic nerve that sees. You cannot see your money in the bank except with your mind. When you draw a check, it is by faith in what you *see,* not with your eyes, but with your mind.

Faith is the most rational thing in the world, because it is based on the greatest of facts and realities. It sees God; it sees Calvary where disease and sin were canceled. It sees the promises of God and His faithfulness. These are more certain than the foundations of a mountain. Faith sees the health and strength given on the cross as already belonging to us. It receives the words: "Himself took our infirmities, and bare our sicknesses," and then acts accordingly. What the eye of faith sees, the *hand* of faith appropriates. It says, "This is mine by virtue of the promise of God." Faith refuses to see anything but God and what He says.

Faith's Glorious Realities

It is a great mistake to suppose a thing is not real because it cannot be seen with natural eyes. Suppose you should trust me to blindfold your eyes and to lead you down the street. The pavement under your feet is just as real as though you could see it. Every time you take a step you are acting a faith that "is the evidence of things not seen" by natural eyes. You see only with your *mind* what I see with my eyes and describe to you. The great spiritual realities and facts that God sees and tells us about are just as real as though we could see them with natural eyes. Because of God, His faithfulness and His promises, faith is the surest ground possible to stand on. To the man who is not enlightened or who does not see the promise of God, it is stepping out into space. To those who have faith in God's Word, it is walking on the foundations of the universe. By merely standing on the naked Word of God, millions of sinners have been "translated out of the kingdom of darkness into the kingdom of God's dear Son." Millions have also been taken from this world to heaven. The promise of God has been better to them than a Jacob's ladder reaching from this world to heaven that could be seen with natural eyes.

Jesus tells us that He came "that they which see not [with the natural eye] might see" with the eye of faith. After ascending to heaven, where He could no longer be seen with the natural eye, He counseled us to anoint our [spiritual] eyes with eye salve that we might see. By doing this, Peter was made to rejoice more over what he saw with his new sight than he ever had over what he saw with the optic nerve. Walking by this better kind of sight is the happiest life possible on earth because of the superiority of what we are constantly beholding: the best things; joy-producing realities. Supernatural joy is always the result of using our better pair of eyes.

It is important to see that real faith is occupied with God's power and mercy, not with human weakness. God invites us to take hold of His strength. He says: "To them that have no might he increaseth strength." He also says: "Let the weak say, I am strong." It is as we obey Him, believing *on the authority of His Word*, that we have His strength. Even when we *feel* weak, His "strength is made perfect in [our] weakness." We must believe what God says in spite of how we feel.

Why Do Some Fail to Receive Healing?

One reason some people are not healed is because they believe what their five senses tell them in the place of believing the Word of God. We should realize that the five senses belong to the *natural* man and that they were given to us to be used for the things of this world. But the things of God cannot be discerned, appropriated and known by the *natural* senses.

No kind of physical sensation, such as pain, weakness or sickness, can ever be a good reason for doubting the fulfillment of any divine promise. How foolish it would be for me to doubt the promise of Christ's second coming because I felt sick or weak, or had a pain. And if a pain is not a good reason for doubting *one* promise, it is not a good reason for doubting *any* promise. God is just as faithful to one promise as to another. If it is foolish to doubt God's promise concerning Christ's second coming because of pain or any disagreeable feeling, it is equally as foolish to doubt God's promise to heal because of these things.

The ground upon which we claim the forgiveness of sins is the fact that Christ bore them "in his own body on the tree" (1 Peter 2:24). We must believe that we are forgiven *before* our feelings can be any different. It is in exactly the same way and on the same ground that we are to appropriate *physical* healing from the Great Physician. The healing of both our souls and bodies is based on the unchangeable truth of Christ's finished work, not on our feelings.

God gives you the redemptive name, "Jehovah-Rapha," thereby saying unto you, "I am the Lord that healeth thee." He wants you to answer with faith, *"Yes, Lord, Thou art the Lord that healeth me."* He wants exactly what He says to be true in your experience. You can make no mistake in saying and steadfastly believing what He says: that He is actually healing you at the present moment. He will continue working until you are "perfectly whole." Faith is saying and believing what God says, and then acting accordingly. The blessings we take by a steadfast faith in God's promises will always materialize.

We Must Not Be Double-Minded

When appropriating the healing Christ has provided, we *must not be double-minded.* James says: "But let him ask in faith, nothing wavering. For he that wavereth is like a wave of the sea driven with the wind and tossed. For let not that man think that he shall receive any thing of the Lord" (James 1:6–7). We must, as it were, behead ourselves and put on "the mind of Christ." This means to see only what He says and to act accordingly. This is implied in our asking "*in faith*." Paul tells us to "put off the old man with his deeds." This includes the old man's habit of thinking only according to the evidence of the five senses. Putting on the new man and having the mind of Christ includes our thinking and believing what is written, and saying, as He did, "It is written." Remember, the "new man" is not governed by the evidence of the senses.

The Word of God Is Powerful

The Bible tells us there is no Word of God without power. Psalm 107:20 tells us: "He sent his word, and healed them." This is His way of healing both our souls and our bodies. I have known of many who have been healed after reading the words in Isaiah 53:5, "With his stripes we *are* healed." They then said, "God says I am healed, and I am going to believe God and not my feelings." By saying and repeating what He says and acting accordingly, even cancers have disappeared. When we steadfastly believe and act our faith in God's Word, nothing can keep the power in the Word from making all things to become exactly as the Word says. All we have to do is firmly believe what the Word says. We need to resolutely refuse to see, believe or think of the things that contradict the Word. We are to take sides with God and believe that all we need for spirit, soul and body is *already ours*. God said to Abraham: "I *have made* thee the father of a multitude." The new name, "Abraham," means "the father of many nations." By taking the new name in faith, the patriarch continually repeated God's Words after Him: "I *AM* the father of a multitude." By thus counting the things that are not as though they were, and giving glory to God in advance, exactly what God said became true.

"As you believe that God has done and given, all He says He has done and given, and as you constantly obey His Word, God makes all the old things leave you and makes all that is of Christ appear in you" (Mrs. C. Nuzum).

God Has Already Given Us All Things

He has given us the things that pertain to life and godliness (2 Peter 1:3). This includes all we need for spirit, soul, and body, for this life and for the life to come. Jesus purchased all this for us. God tells us He *has already* given it to us. Isaiah 53:5 and 1 Peter 2:24 tell us that God *has* healed us. Colossians 1:13 says God *has* delivered us from the power of darkness. In Luke 10:19 Jesus said: "Behold, I give unto you power . . . over all the power of the enemy: and nothing shall by any means hurt you." Romans 6:18 tells us that we are free.

When appropriating all this, God warns us, as in the case of Peter, to never look at our circumstances and feelings. The waves were just as high when Peter walked perfectly on the water as when he sank. While he did not look at them, they could not hinder him. The minute he looked at them, he doubted and went down. The wind also was just as great when Peter walked perfectly, as when he sank. When he did not pay any attention to it, it could not hinder him. God here teaches us that if we are occupied with looking and feeling, instead of with Him and His Word, we will lose all He offers us. On the other hand, by steadfastly refusing to see anything but God and what He says, we shall have and keep everything that He says He has given us.

Mrs. C. Nuzum

"Hold Fast That Thou Hast"

Satan is busy trying to take from us what we take from God. God bids us, "Hold fast that thou hast" (Revelation 3:11). Jesus gave Peter power to walk on the water, but the devil took it from him by getting him to fix his attention on the wind (representing things we feel), and on the waves (representing things we see). Peter had the power, and used it; but lost it by doubting.

Mrs. C. Nuzum

Many lose the manifestation of healing already in operation, by turning their attention from Christ and the Word of God to their feelings. Before taking the step of faith for healing, get this matter fully settled: After taking the step, you are going to see nothing but God and what He says. From that moment doubt should be regarded as out of the question and unreasonable. The evidence upon which you have planted your feet is the Word of God. To watch your feelings or symptoms would be like a farmer digging up his seed to see if it is growing. This would kill the seed at the root. When the true farmer gets his seed into the ground, he says with satisfaction, "I am glad that is *settled*." He believes that the seed has begun its work before he sees it grow. Why not have the same faith in the "Imperishable Seed," the Word of God? Believe that it is already doing its work without waiting to see.

In receiving supernatural healing, the first thing to learn is to cease to be anxious about the condition of the body. You have committed it to the Lord and He has taken the responsibility for your healing. You are to be happy and restful in the matter. You know from His own Word that He takes the responsibility of every case committed to Him. When receiving healing by faith, the body and its sensations are lost sight of, and only the Lord and His promises are in view. Before being conscious of any physical change, faith rejoices and says, "It is written." Jesus won His great victories by saying, "It is written," and believing what was written. Any unfavorable feeling should be regarded as a warning. We should not consider the body, but consider all the more the Lord's promise and be occupied with Him. How much better to be in communion with God and rejoicing in His faithfulness, than to be occupied with a sick body. In this way we have seen multitudes make great spiritual advancement. Others have forfeited sweet communion with God by being occupied with their feelings and symptoms.

How Faith May Be Perfected

In Mark 9:24 we read that the father seeking healing for his child, "cried out, and said with tears, Lord, I believe; help thou mine unbelief." By asking Christ to help him, he received the needed help. He rose to a place of power above the apostles and succeeded where they had failed. In the Greek the Holy Spirit is called the *Paraklete,* which means "helper." Thank God! The Christian can always have His help whenever it is needed. The Holy Spirit is always ready to work in us "that which is well-pleasing in His sight." In a special sense this includes *faith.* "Without faith it is impossible to please Him." Since faith is especially pleasing in His sight, He wants to produce it in our hearts by His Word and by His Spirit. The Holy Spirit is always ready to help every Christian to exercise faith for any blessing God has promised them in His Word. The Bible tells us that Christ is able to save us to the uttermost. This includes particularly His saving us from our unbelief. This is the sin of which the Holy Spirit came to convict us. Therefore, with a resolute purpose hearken only to His Word. Confess to God your unbelief and count on Him for deliverance from it, the same as from any other sin. His grace is always sufficient to cause faith to triumph for the appropriation of any mercy He has provided. The Holy Spirit is always ready to execute for us the fulfillment of any promise God has given.

Why Faith Is Necessary

What is it that constitutes a righteous man? Over and over again we are told that Abraham was *counted righteous.* The story as to *how his righteousness was determined* is very simple. *He believed God and acted accordingly.* He believed and acted as if he had received from God the fulfillment of His promise. To do this is the sum total of righteousness. Nothing can ever be so important and such a privilege as this. It is in this way alone that God's glorious program for the individual and for the Church can be carried out. In no other way can the will and work of God be done by anyone.

Christ was asked the question, "What shall we do that we might work the works of God?" His answer was, "This is the work of God, that ye believe." It is only where He finds the exercise of living faith for the fulfillment of His promises that God can work. Since it is by thus believing God that we are accounted righteous, it is *unbelief* that constitutes us unrighteous. Unbelief is wicked and unrighteous because it hinders and sets aside the divine program, which consists of all that God has promised to do in response to faith. No wonder that it was the sin of unbelief of which God sent the Spirit to convict the world. Anything short of our having a living faith for the will and work of God to be done is unrighteous. Even though we may call it religion, it is something else in the place of His righteousness. Christ's ability to save us unto the uttermost consists in His ability to save us from our unbelief. This is so deadly to the glorious divine program. The Holy Spirit is given to guide us into all truth so that we might believe it, in order that the whole program of God may be carried out. How many there are who believe *in* God, but who do not believe *God* as Abraham did. A steadfast faith for what God has revealed to be His will for us is our whole duty. From every standpoint, this is our greatest privilege. How God would sweep the world with His mighty power if all who profess His name were to set out to discover all divine truth, to believe it with an appropriating faith, and to act accordingly!

Faith in God has a much stronger foundation and a much stronger *Helper* (the Holy Spirit) than either doubt, sin or disease has. The Holy Spirit will free your mind of all doubt if you will rely on Him to do it. Trust Him and keep your attention on the Word of God.

God has provided for the eye of faith to behold glorious and lasting realities. When steadfastly beheld, these *always* become stronger than the cancer or the disease that the optic nerve sees. Doubt and sin and disease can *always* be destroyed by the right use of the "eyes of our understanding." This is the infallible method for our appropriation of all of God's blessings. All the glorious victories of faith recorded in the eleventh chapter of Hebrews were the result of the proper and persistent use of their better sight.

"The law of the Spirit of life" which heals our souls and bodies is much stronger than "the law of sin and death." This law, when not hindered by us, will win every time. Everyone who sets himself to obtain the benefits of the Atonement has an infinitely capable Helper. His power, when relied on, can never fail. As God's grace is stronger than sin, *so Christ's healing virtue is much more powerful than the strength of any*

disease. And the evidence God gives us for faith (His own Word), when it occupies the mind, is much stronger than any evidence Satan can give us to make us doubt.

What Is the Exercise of Faith?

Jesus said to the man with the withered hand, "Stretch forth thy hand." Christ first gives faith, then calls it to its wondrous exercise. The man stretched forth his hand in reliance on divine strength, and it was made whole. As we put forth effort, in reliance on God, to do what without Him is impossible, God meets us with divine power. The thing is done independent of nature. In anything that God calls us to do, "All things are possible [not to him that feels able in himself, but] to him that *believeth.*" We see this man's ability not in himself, but *in Christ.* Every part of salvation is contained in Him. "I can do *all* things *through Christ* which strengtheneth me." Through our union with Christ, the true Vine, the strength is *already* ours. But it must be put to use. It was the man's effort to put forth his hand that opened the way for the healing touch to be given and the divine life to flow. Although begun in the natural, this *act* of faith became a way of entrance for the supernatural to meet the man's need. By virtue of the divine power imparted, it led at once to an action wholly supernatural. It led to an exercise of the body not possible according to former conditions. It was an act independent of natural forces and wholly dependent on God.

The act of faith is not only a *physical* act; it includes the exercise of the *heart* and *mind* toward God. The full exercise of faith means that we think faith, speak faith, act faith. This brings the manifestation of all that faith takes according to the promise of the Word. You may be asking, "How can one exercise faith for the healing of blindness or of an affliction that does not interfere with the motion of the body?" To the blind man Jesus said: "Go wash in the pool of Siloam." This act gave the man an opportunity to exercise faith in heart, mind and body. It was the same with Naaman, with the ten lepers and with the centurion. In each case they went relying on the Word of Christ. They believed the healing was theirs before it was manifested to sight.

You might deposit a thousand dollars in the bank and come and tell me that you had made me a present of that amount. If I believed you, I would act my faith and draw checks on the bank as I needed the money. I have not seen the money in the bank, but it is just as much mine as though I saw it and had it in my hands. Just so healing for our souls and bodies is in Christ. God has made the treasury of all He is. Sickness, from which I have been redeemed, does not belong to me, but healing does. Therefore, I begin to check on healing. How? By attempting in His name what I cannot do without Him. This is acting faith; checking health and strength from the bank of God. It is counting on something we do not see or feel, but which we know from God's own Word is ours. In the same way, the money in the bank is ours, although we do not see or feel it.

The Girdled Tree

Someone may ask: "How can I say that I am healed, when I see disease in the body and am conscious of pain?" There is an illustration in nature sometimes given which makes the truth clearer. One method of killing a tree is to girdle it, and when we see a tree girdled we think of it as a dead tree. Still its foliage is fresh and green for a while and gives evidence of life. The natural eye sees life. The mind's eye, which has knowledge beyond what nature beholds, sees death. In time the leaves wither and fall, and death, which the mind's eye saw from the first, becomes manifest to the senses. So it is when we take healing for the body. As we claim the *Word* of promise, in faith receiving a finished work, the "sword of the Spirit" strikes the death blow to disease. For a little time symptoms may remain; but the eye of faith which beholds the Crucified One sees disease canceled and health given. "Calling the things which be not as though they were," the new life is manifested in the body. That which the eye of faith saw from the first as the truth becomes manifest to the senses. Faith sees God in His love and omnipotence making good the Word.

From "Gems of Truth on Divine Healing"

Being governed by natural sight is unscientific because it does not take into account all the facts. It overlooks the greatest and best of facts. Healing by natural means only is unscientific because it overlooks important facts. It overlooks the supernatural agency in disease as well as the privilege of the supernatural in its recovery.

We thank God for the thousands who have made great spiritual advancement while receiving healing in this way. The process of faith that brings the healing is a far greater blessing than the healing itself. Many throughout the Scriptures became famous for having faith as a result of seeking God for what we call *temporal* blessings. When we have learned the process of faith for receiving healing, we have learned how to receive everything else God promises us in His Word. The Church could win millions for the service of God, and make them fighters of "the good fight of faith," by offering to them the healing of Christ purchased for them. May you, dear Reader, by learning to be healed in this way, advance into a life of faith and usefulness in the Kingdom of God.

8

How to Have Your Prayers Answered

The Past Tenses of God's Word

It is important that those who seek for the mercies of God see that appropriating faith is *taking* and *using* what God offers to us. *Hope is expecting* a blessing some time in the *future. Faith* is *taking now* what God offers.

We are to believe what God says He has done for us and act on it. We are to take our blood-bought liberty just as the slaves of the South did after the Emancipation Proclamation by Abraham Lincoln.

The Gospel is a worldwide emancipation proclamation of liberty from service and bondage to the old tyrant master of sin and sickness, the devil. When Jesus said "It is finished," He meant that the work was done. As God sees it, it is completed. God expects us to reckon as done what Jesus says was done. The past tenses of God's Word mean a settled, sealed and final decision of His will.

In Galatians 3:13 we read "Christ *hath* [past tense] redeemed us from the curse of the law, being made a curse for us." God has put our redemption from the curse of the law in the past tense. We receive our deliverance when we do the same. In the 28th chapter of Deuteronomy, we see that the curse of the law includes all diseases.

In God's Word we read, "Surely he *hath* [past tense] borne our sicknesses and carried our pain. . . . Himself took [past tense] our infirmities, and bare our sicknesses. . . . By whose stripes *ye were* healed."

God wants us all to appropriate the past tenses of His Word regarding His redemption of our souls and bodies from sickness and disease. He wants us to go forth in obedience acting as if we believed Him. When God puts a promise in the past tense, He thus authorizes and expects us to do the same. Nothing short of this is appropriating faith.

In Mark 11:24 Jesus authorizes and commands us to put the reception of the blessing we pray for in the past tense. He says that *when we ask* for the promises that He offers, we should believe that we *have received* them, and that we *shall* have them. We are to continue to believe that God gave us what we asked for when we prayed. We are to continue to praise and thank Him for what He has given us. It is *after* we believe we have received what we ask for, after we believe He has heard our prayer, that God goes to work. *Then* the imperishable seed, His Word, begins to grow.

The farmer has to get the sowing of his seed into the past tense before it is possible to reap a harvest. The permanent receiving of God's Word, the imperishable seed, has to be sown into the "good ground" of our heart. It is necessary to get the sowing into the past tense before the seed *can* begin its work.

Believing that God has already heard our prayer before the blessing is manifested is the good soil in which the imperishable seed, His Word, grows and bears fruit. Believing that God *has* heard our prayer gets the seed into the ground, and *then,* (and not before) it goes to work.

At the grave of Lazarus Jesus said, *while Lazarus was still dead,* "I thank thee that thou *hast* heard me." The sick who pray for healing are to say before the healing materializes, "Father, I thank Thee that Thou *hast* heard me." The prayer of *faith* is believing our prayer is heard before the answer materializes—*before* the answer is manifested. "This is the confidence that we have in him, that, if we ask any thing according to his will, he heareth us: And if we know that he hears us, whatsoever we ask, we *know* that we *have* the petitions that we desired of him."

It is *before* having experienced or being conscious of any change whatsoever that faith rejoices and says, "It is written." When we ask for healing, we are to say on the authority of God's Word, "I thank Thee that Thou hast heard me."

Faith refuses to see (as reason for doubting) anything contrary to the Word of God. It sees the health and strength bequeathed to us as already belonging to us because of the death of the Testator. By His death the will is in force. Jesus says to us, "As thou *hast* believed [past tense], *so* be it done unto thee."

With our natural eyes we see only the temporal and inferior things of earth, but with the enlightened eyes of our understanding we behold the superior, satisfying and lasting realities of God's spiritual and eternal Kingdom.

God said to Abraham, "A father of many nations have I made thee" (past tense). Since God put this promise in the past tense, Abraham did the same and acted his faith by taking his new name, "Abraham," which means "the father of a multitude."

A man put a certain amount of money in the pocket of his wife's coat telling her he had done so. He asked her if she believed him. She replied, "Certainly I do" and began to plan how she would spend it. She actually had this money before she saw it. Why should we believe the bare word of *others* and demand proof from God?

If someone should deed you a home that you have never seen, you actually have a home before you see it. "Faith is . . . the evidence [title deed] of things not [yet] seen." A deed makes a home so much yours that you can sell it without ever seeing it. Faith is believing you *have* what God says you have and acting accordingly before you either feel or see that you have it.

God said to Joshua, "See, I *have* given into thine hand Jericho." Joshua and his men put this victory in the past tense as God had done, and the walls of Jericho fell down flat while they were acting their faith.

Jesus said to the ten lepers who asked for mercy, "Go show yourselves unto the priests." His words unto them were as much as to say, "I have given you my Word that it is done." They knew the law of the leper and therefore what His command meant. They put their healing in the past tense before seeing it, and it was manifested while they were acting their faith.

Jonah put his deliverance in the past tense, called his symptoms "lying vanities" and sacrificed with the voice of thanksgiving while he was still in the stomach of the great fish. It worked.

The reason thousands are not getting what they pray for is that they are keeping their blessing in the future tense. This is only *hope* and not *faith,* which *takes* the blessings *now.*

Were the gifts of God for soul and body merely *promised* gifts, we would have to wait for the Promiser to fulfill His promises, and the responsibility would be on Him. But all of God's blessings are *offered* gifts as well as promised, and therefore need to be *accepted*. The responsibility for their transfer is ours. This clears *God* of all responsibility for any failures.

The only reason you were not saved a year earlier than you were is that you did not take what God had provided and was offering to you. God was not making you wait; you were making Him wait.

Some say, "God will heal me in His own good time." This is only *hope* and not faith. Faith *takes* what God offers *now*.

9

The Faith That Takes

What things soever ye desire, when ye pray, believe that ye
receive them, and ye shall have them.

Mark 11:24

Faith—A Title Deed

"Faith is . . . the evidence [or title deed] of things not seen"
(Hebrews 11:1). In Jeremiah a title deed is repeatedly spoken
of as "the evidence." Your deed is "the evidence" or proof that
you own your home. Faith is the title deed to what you have
not yet seen. When you have been given a deed to a home,
which you have not yet seen, you already have a home before
you see it. Jesus repeatedly said, "He that believeth, hath."
Moffatt's translation of Hebrews 11:1 reads: "Faith means
that we are . . . convinced of what we do not see."

In Mark 11:24 Jesus commands us to believe we "have
received" the things we pray for at the time we pray, without

waiting to see or feel them. On this condition He promises, "Ye *shall* have them." Faith for the healing of your body is the same as faith for forgiveness. You are to believe, on the authority of God's Word, that you were forgiven before you felt forgiven. Nothing else is faith, for faith is the evidence of things *not seen*. As soon as the blessing we take by faith is *manifested*, faith for that blessing ends.

If you are the beneficiary in a rich man's will, you are already wealthy the moment the rich man dies, though you have not yet seen any of the money. Just so, everything bequeathed to us in our Lord's last will and testament is already ours by virtue of the death of Jesus, the Testator. Faith is simply using what belongs to us.

Healing is the same as with forgiveness. We are to believe we "have received" healing at the time we pray, before seeing or feeling it. This is the "confidence" that the Holy Spirit, in Hebrews 10:35–36, tells us not to cast away. The reason is that this confidence "hath great recompence of reward." Peter tells us that it is the testing of this faith (the faith that we "have received") that is "more precious than gold."

We are to believe that our prayer is granted at the time we pray, that we already have what we prayed for before we see it. This is the "confidence" referred to in 1 John 5:14–15: "We *know* that we *have* the petitions that we desired of him."

The fig tree, which Jesus cursed, dried up, not from the leaves that could be seen, but "from the roots," which were out of sight. By looking at the leaves, the death of the tree could not be detected at first.

Our "Emancipation Proclamation"

Calvary was our "emancipation proclamation" from everything outside of the will of God. We are simply to believe what God says He has done for us, and act on it. We are to take our blood-bought liberty just as the slaves of the South did after the Emancipation Proclamation by Abraham Lincoln. Suppose the slaves had judged by the evidence of the senses. Suppose they said: "I don't feel different; I can't see any change; all my surroundings are just the same as they were." Would that be faith? It was *faith* only when they acted on the freedom, which was already theirs.

By believing and acting on the Word of God, everything that belongs to us in Christ becomes available at once. To accept any contrary physical evidence in preference to the Word of God is to nullify the Word, as far as you are concerned. Faith is believing what God says in the face of the contrary evidence of the senses. We are to be "steadfast" in resisting, as reasons for doubting, everything contrary to the Word of God. Faith means that we have left the realm of the senses.

If a friend should deposit a hundred thousand dollars in the bank to your credit and bring you the passbook and a checkbook, you wouldn't examine your empty pocketbook to see how much money you have. You would examine your passbook. The Bible is the Christian's passbook. God has deposited in Christ all I need. It is already mine. To neglect it is not a proper attitude toward God. A right attitude toward God and His promises will bring about their fulfillment.

You have to receive Christ before experiencing any of the wonderful results of receiving Him. Christ comes *first*; *afterward* come the results. We receive healing, divine life and strength and every other promised blessing in exactly the same way we received Christ and forgiveness. Since forgiveness is invisible, how do you receive it? Answer: by faith in God's Word. Why not receive divine healing, life and strength in the same way?

With every blessing that is received *by faith*, you must have it before you see and before it is manifested. Otherwise it would not be received *by faith*. Faith is "the evidence of things not seen." The ten lepers already had healing in its unmanifested form when they started on their way to show the priest they were healed. Their healing was manifested while they were acting their faith. God's announcement, "I am the Lord that healeth thee," is to be received as the voice of God. It is to be believed as a present-tense fact and evaluated according to its cost.

The Six Senses

Perfume is nonexistent to the sense of hearing. What we take by faith according to Mark 11:24 is, at first, nonexistent to the five natural senses. You do not doubt the existence of what you *see* because you can't *smell* or *taste* or *hear* it. Then why doubt the existence of what you have taken by faith (the sixth sense) because you can't *yet see or feel it*? The five natural senses belong to "the *natural* man." Paul tells us that he "receiveth not the things . . . of God." It is only by our *sixth* sense, faith, that we can see, take and hold on to the blessings God offers to us until they are fully manifested. To consult our natural senses for evidence that our prayer has been granted is as ridiculous as trying to see with our ears or to hear with our eyes.

All of our six senses work independently of each other. You *see* what you can't hear; you hear what you can't see, etc. In the same way, you have by faith what is, at first, nonexistent to the natural senses. It is important to see that the contrary evidence of the senses is no reason for doubting. The evidences on which faith rests are still perfect. It is only faith when we are believing in the face of the contrary evidence of the senses. Abraham received and believed the Word of God in the face of *nature's* evidence to the *impossibility*.

You must already have perfume, before you can smell it. You must already have food, before you can taste it. You must also already have the healing, before you can feel it. Faith receives forgiveness and healing. It then praises God for them when there is nothing to praise Him for as far as the five senses are concerned.

Jesus said, "I thank thee that thou hast heard me," when the raising of Lazarus was yet in an unmanifested form. Before we see or feel any change, we are to believe that our prayer for healing is granted. We are to say as Jesus did, "I thank Thee that Thou hast heard me." The angels at Dothan were already present before they became visible to the servant of Elisha. The ability God gave him to *see* these angels did not create them.

God works while we maintain the mental habit of faith; "While we look not at the things which are seen, but at the things which are not seen" (2 Corinthians 4:18). We look at God: at His promises, His faithfulness, His justice, etc. Faith has to do only with the unseen and unfelt. As soon as what we have taken by faith is manifested to the senses, it ceases to be faith.

The Right Mental Attitude

No person who allows his mind to be ruled by his senses can have victorious faith. The mind that is ruled by the senses lives in a realm of uncertainty. Until God's Word gains mastery over your mind, your mind will be swayed by feelings and by things you see or hear, rather than by the Word of God. The mind and thoughts of those seeking healing must be renewed. They must be brought into harmony with the mind of God as revealed in the Bible and pointed out in this book. Faith for God's promised blessings is the result of knowing and acting on God's Word. The right mental attitude, or the "renewed mind" (Romans 12:2), makes steadfast faith possible to all. God always heals when He can get the right cooperation.

Having before Seeing

I put a certain amount of money in Mrs. Bosworth's coat pocket. Later, I told her what I had done, asking her if she believed me. She said, "Of course I do," and thanked me for it. She actually had this money before she saw it. Why should we believe the bare word of *others* and demand visible proof from God?

Continue to believe that God gave you what you asked for when you prayed, thanking and praising Him for what He has given, and it will always materialize. This always puts God to work. So many are waiting for God to heal them, when He is waiting for them to take what He is offering them. How trying it would be to a friend who offered you a gift if you cried and begged for it, and then kept him waiting for you to take it!

Let me put this in another way. Jesus commands us to believe we "have received" the things we pray for at the time we pray and before they take visible form. It is clear that they exist in two forms: first, *invisible*; afterward, *visible*. First, "believe that *ye have received* them [in their invisible form] and *ye shall* have them [in their visible or material form]."

We have them *first*, in the *faith* realm, *afterward* in the *sense* realm. Jesus, in Mark 11:24, commands us as soon as we pray to believe that we "have received" (in its invisible form) what we pray for. Then, He changes it into its visible or material form. The ten lepers each had their healing in its invisible form while they were on their way to show the priest their healing in its *visible* and material form.

When Jesus said, "I thank Thee that Thou *hast* heard Me," the raising of Lazarus was complete in the faith realm before it was seen. A few moments later it was manifested in the sense or material form. In the same way, we are to believe that we already have our complete healing in its invisible form before God changes it into its visible or material form. The fact that faith is "the evidence [or title deed] of things *not seen*" proves that we must already have the things for which we pray. We receive them first in their invisible form, before God *can* change them into their *visible or manifested form*.

The entire eleventh chapter of Hebrews records the actions of God's saints in the faith realm *before* the results of their faith took visible form. All the acts of faith are in the realm of the yet unseen. Believing that we have received the things we pray for at the time we pray is the "confidence," which is to be steadfast. We have unwavering faith until God changes the blessings we have taken, from their *invisible* to their visible form.

Walking by faith is walking by the kind of sight that sees and is occupied with eternal things. It sees God, His promises, His faithfulness and the many other perfect reasons for faith. It was *believing without seeing* that gave Peter "joy unspeakable and full of glory." Nothing he had ever seen gave him as much joy as he now had by believing without seeing.

The sacrifice of praise and the giving of thanks is continually done in the *faith* realm. This is before our blessings have been changed into their visible form. Jonah called his symptoms "lying vanities" and sacrificed with the voice of thanksgiving while he was still in the stomach of the great fish. The Israelites sang praises on their way to battle.

10

Our Confession

Many people fail to receive what they pray for because of a lack of understanding about *confession*. In Hebrews 3:1 Christianity is called a "profession." The Greek word here translated "profession" is the same as the one usually translated "confession."

What It Means

The word *confession* in the Greek language means "saying the same thing." It means to believe and say what God says about our sins, our sicknesses and everything else included in our redemption. Confession is an *affirmation* of a Bible truth we have embraced. Confession is simply believing with our hearts and repeating with our lips God's own declaration of what we are in Christ.

The Holy Spirit in 1 Peter 2:24 says: "By whose stripes ye were healed." We are to believe and say the same thing. When our affirmation is the Word of God, He watches over it to make it good (Jeremiah 1:12).

Confession is faith's way of expressing itself.

"The High Priest of Our Confession"

In Hebrews 3:1 we are commanded to consider the "Apostle and High Priest of our profession, Christ Jesus." When it is in accordance with God's Word, Jesus, our High Priest, acts in our behalf according to what we confess.

Paul tells us that he preached "the Word of faith." He said, "If thou shalt confess with thy mouth *the Lord* Jesus, and shalt believe in thine heart that God hath raised him from the dead, thou shalt be saved. For with the heart man believeth unto righteousness; and with the mouth confession is made unto salvation" (Romans 10:9–10).

The Relation of Confession to Manifestation

Notice here that the confession, saying the same thing that God says, is by *faith*. It is believing and confessing *before* experiencing the result.

The confession comes *first*, and *then* Jesus our High Priest responds with the new birth. It is not salvation unto confession, but confession unto salvation. Confession comes before salvation. There is no such thing as salvation without confession.

Faith is acting on God's Word. This always puts God to work fulfilling His promise.

What Are We to Confess?

Few Christians today have recognized the place confession holds in God's plan for our appropriation of His blessings. Whenever the word *confession* is used, many instinctively think of confessing sin, weakness and failure. This is only the negative side of this great question. Our *negative* confession of *sin* was only to open the way for the *positive* confession

151

"unto salvation." This covers a whole lifetime of believing with our heart and saying with our lips everything God says to us in His promises.

Confessing unto salvation in its *initial* form, and then in each of its *successive* forms, is essential. We confess God's Word first in the form of the new birth, then in the form of every blessing that is promised to us. The Christian is to act on every phase of his salvation that he knows about. We are to believe with the heart and confess with our mouth to the extent of the "Word of faith," which Paul preached. He preached "all the counsel of God." He preached "the unsearchable riches of Christ." He said that he "kept back nothing that was profitable" to them.

All that Jesus did in His substitutionary work is the private property of the individual for whom Jesus did it. Throughout our Christian life God wants us to believe with our heart and say with our lips all He says we are in Christ. We are not to ignore or neglect our *legal* standing in Christ. It is the basis for the acts of faith that puts God to work fulfilling His Word to us. We are to confess or whisper in our own heart, "In Him I am complete." When we know that God in His Word says, "I am the Lord that healeth thee," we are to believe it and confess it with our lips. Christ will act as our High Priest and make it good.

We are to confess that Calvary was our "emancipation proclamation," freeing us from everything outside the will of God, and act accordingly. We are to confess that our sicknesses were laid on Christ and that we are redeemed from the curse of disease. "Let him that is weak say, I am strong," for "the Lord is my strength."

Our confession includes:

The whole of Scripture truth
All that His sacrifice provided

All that His High Priesthood covers
The whole of God's revealed will

We are to confess that our redemption is complete. Satan's dominion is ended; Calvary has freed us. We are to believe that we are free on the basis of our emancipation proclamation, never on the basis of our feelings, or on the evidences of our senses.

Remission is the wiping out of everything connected with the old life. We are a "new creature: old things have passed away; and all things are become new." We are to make continual confession of our redemption from Satan's dominion.

Of course we are not to say to others that our healing is fully manifested before it is. God does not say that. But you can say to those who ask you, "I am standing on the Word of God."

Wrong Confession

We never rise above our confession. A negative confession will lower us to the level of that confession. It is what we confess with our lips that really controls us. Our confession imprisons us if it is negative, or sets us free if it is positive. Many are always telling of their failings and their lack of faith. Invariably they go to the level of their confession. Confessing a lack of faith increases doubt. Every time you confess doubts and fears, you confess your faith in Satan and deny the ability and grace of God. When you confess doubt, you are imprisoned with your own words. Proverbs 6:2 says "Thou art snared with the words of thy mouth, thou art taken [captive] with the words of thy mouth." When we doubt His Word, it is because we believe something else that is contrary to that Word. Wrong confession shuts the Father out and lets Satan in.

We are to refuse to have anything to do with wrong confessions. When we realize that we will never rise above our confession, we are getting to the place where God can use us.

Disease gains the ascendancy when you confess the testimony of your senses. Feelings and appearances have no place in the realm of faith. Confessing disease is like signing for a package that the express company has delivered. Satan then has the receipt from you showing you have accepted it. Don't accept anything that Satan brings. "Give no place to the devil."

First Peter 4:11: "If any man speak, let him speak as the oracles of God." In Ephesians 4:29 we are commanded to speak only "that which is good to the use of edifying." We are not to testify for the adversary. We are to *act* faith, *speak* faith and *think* faith.

In Philippians 4:8 the Holy Spirit says, "Finally, brethren, whatsoever things are true [the Word is], whatsoever things are honest, whatsoever things are just, whatsoever things are pure, whatsoever things are lovely, whatsoever things are of good report; if there be any virtue, and if there be any praise, *think* on these things."

The Holy Spirit says in Proverbs, as a man "thinketh in his heart so is he." In 2 Corinthians 10:4–5, the Holy Spirit says, "The weapons of our warfare are . . . mighty . . . bringing into captivity every thought to the obedience of Christ." We are to cast down imaginations (reasonings) and give the Word of God its place in our minds and on our lips.

The Mind of Christ

Jesus remembers when He bore your sicknesses. The Holy Spirit commands, "Forget not all his benefits, who forgiveth all thine iniquities, who healeth all thy diseases."

God's spiritual and physical transformations are to come to us "by the renewing of our mind." Romans 12:1–2: ". . . present your *bodies* [the home or laboratory of the five senses] a living sacrifice. . . . Be ye transformed by the renewing of your mind, that ye may prove what is that good, and acceptable, and perfect, will of God."

A spiritual law that few recognize is that our confession rules us. It is what we confess with our lips that really dominates our inner being. Make your lips do their duty. Refuse to allow them to destroy the effectiveness of God's Word in your case. Some confess with their lips but deny in their hearts. They say, "Yes, the Word is true," but in their hearts they say, "It is not true in my case." The confession of your lips has no value as long as your heart repudiates it.

Hold Fast Your Confession

Hebrews 4:14 (ASV): "Having then a great high priest, who hath passed through the heavens, Jesus the Son of God, let us *hold fast* our confession." This is the confession of our faith in the redemptive work that God wrought in Christ.

I am told to *hold fast* to the confession of the absolute integrity of the Bible. I am told to *hold fast* to the confession of the work of Christ in all its phases. I am told to *hold fast* to the confession that "God is the strength of my life." I am told to *hold fast* to the confession that "surely He hath borne my sicknesses and carried my diseases" and that "by his stripes I am healed."

God says this, and we are to believe and *say* the same things. We are to know what our rights are as revealed by the Word, and then *hold fast* to our confession of those rights.

When you know that Christ "took our infirmities and bore our sicknesses," *hold fast* to your confession of this truth.

When you read "greater is he that is in you than he that is in the world," *hold fast* to this confession.

We are to *hold fast* our confession of what Christ has done *for us*, in order that it may be done *in us*.

We are to *hold fast* to the confession of our redemption from Satan's dominion.

We are to *hold fast* to our confession in the face of all contrary evidence.

God declares that "with his stripes we are healed." I am to confess what God says about my sickness, and *hold fast* to this confession. I am to recognize the absolute truthfulness of these words in advance of any visible change. I am to act on these words and thank Him for the fact that He laid my sickness on Christ the same as He did my sins.

Healing is always in response to faith's testimony. Some fail when things get difficult *because they lose their confession*. Disease, like sin, is defeated by our confession of the Word. Make your lips do their duty; fill them with the Word. Make them say what God says about your sickness. Don't allow them to say anything to the contrary.

Believing God's Word with our heart implies our having "put off the old man" with his habit of judging by the evidence of the senses. Faith regards all contrary symptoms as "lying vanities" as Jonah did, and puts the Word in the place of the senses.

Our only problem is to keep in harmony with God's Word and not allow the senses to usurp the place of the Word. We cease to agree with doubting Thomas who says, "Except I shall see, I will not believe." We are to prove Christ's own words, "Blessed are they that have not seen, and yet believe." The Word is lifeless until faith is breathed into it on your lips. *Then* it becomes a supernatural force. Make your lips harmonize with the Word of God.

Christ's High Priestly ministry meets our every need from the moment of our new birth until we enter heaven. Why are we to hold fast our confession?

- Because Christ is the *High Priest* of our Confession (Hebrews 4:14–16).
- Because He is a *great* High Priest.
- Because He is a *merciful* High Priest.
- Because He is touched with the *feeling* of our infirmities.
- Because He ever liveth "to make intercession for us." He is always ready to give us "*grace* to help in time of need."

Our Success Is Assured

Because Jesus is "the High Priest of our Confession," our success is assured. When you confess that "by His stripes I am healed" and hold on to your confession, no disease can stand before you. Just thank the Father and praise Him whenever a need confronts you that is covered by redemption, and it is yours. Faith is thanking God from the heart for healing that has not yet been manifested. We are as sure of this as if it were manifested.

The confession of your lips that has grown out of faith in your heart will absolutely defeat the adversary in every conflict. Christ's Words broke the power of demons and healed the sick. They do the same thing today when we believe and confess them. The Word will heal you if you continually confess it. God will make your body obey your confession of His Word; for no Word of God is void of power (Luke 1:37).

If I dare say that Psalm 34:10 is true, "But they that seek the LORD shall not want any good thing," and stand by my confession, God will make good all I have confessed.

Nothing will establish you and build your faith as quickly as confession:

- Confess it in your heart first.
- Confess it out loud in your room.
- Say it over and over again.
- Say it until your spirit and your words agree.
- Say it until your whole being swings into harmony and into line with the Word of God.

Christ's Words are filled with Himself, and as we act on them, they fill us with Christ. We are to obey the Word as we would obey Jesus if He stood visibly in our presence.

Confessing Christ as Lord

When coming to God for salvation in its initial form, and then in every other form afterward, one thing is necessary. Our confession of, and surrender to, Christ's *lordship* is required. The Holy Spirit says in Colossians 2:6, "As ye have therefore received Christ Jesus *the Lord*, so walk ye in him." Romans 14:9: "For to this end Christ both died, and rose, and revived, that he might be *Lord* both of the dead and living." Appropriating faith for the fulfillment of any promise implies our surrender to His *lordship*. It is while we are surrendered to Him *as Lord* over our lives, that He is ready to:

- Heal us
- Baptize us with the Spirit
- Give us *zoe*—God's own life in abundance

158

- Be within us a fountain springing up unto everlasting life
- Make our legal standing our experience
- Manifest His Person in the form of every blessing promised
- Be Himself our strength, our portion, our all
- Give us the unlimited use of His name
- Enable us to cast out demons in His name
- Anoint us for preaching
- Enable us to lay our hands on the sick for their recovery

Your success and usefulness in the world is going to be measured by your confession and by the tenacity with which you "hold fast" to that confession under all circumstances. God can be no bigger in you than you confess Him to be. In the face of every need, confess that the Lord is your Shepherd and that you do not want.

᧒

Most of the thoughts expressed in this sermon I have brought together, by permission, from the writings of the late Reverend E. W. Kenyon. He was the author of "The Father and His Family," "The Wonderful Name of Jesus," "Two Kinds of Life," "Jesus the Healer," "In His Presence," "Two Kinds of Love," "Two Kinds of Faith," "Two Kinds of Righteousness" and "Kenyon's Living Poems."

11

Fullness of God's Life
The Secret of Victory

Without a divine revelation I cannot tell a person the specific reason why his or her prayer for the fulfillment of a divine promise is delayed. I can, however, point you to a most wonderful truth. This is the most vital of all truths that God has revealed. It is the only cure for all our ailments. A delay in receiving healing for instance is, in one sense, good news. The good news is that we can have more of the "Life of God."

There are four Greek words in the New Testament, translated "life." One of these means "manner of life"; another means "human life"; another "behavior"; but the Greek word for the kind of life that Jesus brought to the world is *zoe*. This is translated "eternal life" and the "Life of God." "Eternal life" is the actual Life of the Eternal One Himself.

The gospel of John opens with the word *zoe*. This word is found in the New Testament one hundred and thirty times.

John 10:10 tells us that man was to have a right to an abundance of a new kind of life, "God's own Life." It is new, of course, only in the sense of human possession.

The Life That Lives Itself

Many ministers today major on the "manner of life" and "behavior" rather than *zoe*, the "Life of God." When received in sufficient measure, *zoe* lives itself. Paul prayed for Christians, already filled with the Spirit, that they "might be filled with all the fullness of God." This shows that *zoe* is God Himself, and all we have of it is an unsevered part of the "Life of God." The way to be "full of faith" is to be full of that kind of Life, which "believeth all things." The way to be full of divine love is to be full of the "Life of God," who is love.

"All things are possible" to *zoe*. When it is received in sufficient measure, it can fulfill in us any promise or any requirement in the Bible. To fulfill in us all that the Bible requires or promises is precisely what the "Life of God" in us was to accomplish. By receiving enough of the "Life of God," we can be made "more than conquerors," "spirit, soul and body." God wants to do in us, all that He did in Christ *for* us.

Zoe received in sufficient measure transforms us "from glory to glory into the image of Christ." It turns belief into knowledge. It is the source of all the divine graces. It gives us God's wisdom. It overcomes "the world, the flesh and the devil." It works in us "that which is well-pleasing in his sight."

It is by filling us with His own Life that God Himself becomes our life, our peace, our righteousness, our purity, our strength and our health. He becomes the Preserver of "our whole spirit, soul and body," our zeal, our joy, our faith.

Through His Life, He is our Guide, our Teacher, our satisfaction and our "everything that pertains to life and godliness."

God's Blessings Are a Part of Himself

By filling us with more and more of His Life, God wants to manifest Himself in us in the form of every spiritual blessing He has promised. This is the miracle and the genius of Christianity. Romans 5:10 tells us, that we are "saved by his life." This is true for both soul and body.

It is impossible to measure up to God's purpose for our prayer life without being full of that Life that "ever liveth to make intercession." In other words, it is when *zoe* inspires our prayers that we can ask what we will and receive it. *Zoe*, the "Life of God," is the healer of soul and body. Divine healing, divine life and divine strength are Christ *Himself* "made manifest in our mortal flesh." The fullness of this new life is better than the healing it produces. David said, "The *Lord* is my portion"; "the Lord is my strength." His blessings were God manifesting *Himself* in these various forms. God gives each of us spiritual blessings by giving us Himself; our blessings are a part of God.

Jesus said, "I am the vine and ye are the branches." The Vine's life is in the branches. "The life of the branches is a part of the life of the vine." It is Christ's will that all the branches shall be *full* of His own Life. When we are *full* of *zoe*, we are one with God just as the bay is one with the ocean because the tides flow into the bay. Paul says, "They that are joined to the Lord are one spirit." That is to say, our spirit and His Spirit are blended into one. This truth provides us with one of the answers to the question, Why am I not healed?

I have heard Christians express their reasons for wanting to be filled with the Spirit. It seems to me that every Christian in the world would pray until they were filled with the Spirit. Many do not know the many glorious reasons why the Holy Spirit wants them to be filled with Himself. One of His reasons is that He wants to be unhindered in His wonderful work of continually quickening our whole spirit, soul and body. In John 6:63, Jesus said, "It is the spirit that quickeneth," or giveth Life. He is spoken of in Romans as "the Spirit of life." All life is due to the direct action of the Holy Spirit. It is His work to impart to us continually the actual Life of Jesus. Jesus is the true source of Life for both the souls and bodies of God's children. His work of quickening or increasing the divine life in our spirit, soul and body is hindered or limited when we are anything less than *full* of the Spirit.

Jesus said that He came, not only that we might have Life, but that we might have it "more abundantly." We cannot have His Life in the measure that He desires unless we are filled with the Spirit. The abiding, which Christ commanded, keeps us filled with the Spirit. This removes from us all hindrances to the Spirit's constant quickening. In the 119th Psalm, David used the word *quicken* eleven times. He knew that more Life is the cure, the only cure, for all our ailments. It is good to know what we pray for. David desired quickening, more Life, increased Life. He therefore sought that blessing that is the root of all the rest. He prayed, "Quicken me after thy lovingkindness." We need never fear anything that lovingkindness does. Nothing else is so good. Lovingkindness itself cannot do us a greater service than by making us to have "life more abundantly."

"According to Thy Word"

In the 25th verse of Psalm 119, David prayed, "Quicken thou me according to thy word." Thank God we can all pray with faith and get the answer every day. This is a comprehensive and inspired prayer, "Quicken thou me according to thy word." Notice that the quickening is, as David said, "*according to thy word.*" The Holy Spirit inspired the Word of God. It is His own blueprint from which He works while carrying on His great work of quickening. To be quickened "according to God's Word" means to be full of His Life in the entire range of our complex being: body, soul and spirit.

God has made Christ the treasury of all that He is. In Him is "all the fullness of the Godhead bodily." We can be full of everything that the Vine contains. The abiding branch not only has life, but is *full* of life all the time. It is by the Spirit's fullness and the consequent unhindered quickening that we are "preserved," as Paul says, "spirit, soul and body." Paul says the Spirit will "quicken also your mortal body." In 2 Corinthians 4:11 we have the words, "that the life also of Jesus might be made manifest in our mortal flesh." If you need healing from Christ, wait on God for the Spirit to quicken you to the extent that Mark 11:24 shall be fulfilled in you. This is exactly what the Divine Quickener wants to do for you.

Let us pray every day, "Quicken Thou me (give me more Life) *according to Thy Word.*" This is according to every revelation we find in the Bible that shows us how God wants us to be. Every time you discover in the Word more than what God requires, rejoice. Be encouraged. It is the work of the Spirit, not your work, to quicken you just to that extent. Let this prayer be your first prayer every day; it is the condition of a thousand other blessings. It is God's way of "fulfilling in you all the good pleasure of His goodness." The Holy Spirit wants to quicken us to the extent that everything He has revealed concerning us in God's Word shall be fulfilled in us.

In the fiftieth verse of this Psalm 119, David says, "Thy word hath quickened me." The Spirit quickens us according to our trust in God's Word. This is to the extent of every promise or command that we find from time to time in the Word of God. This quickening will be, as Paul says, "from glory to glory." God's words "are spirit and life" and they accomplish exactly what they reveal. When we pray to be quickened "according to His *Word*," we know that we are praying according to His *will*. We can, therefore, obtain the answer. "According to His Word" means according to both His promises and His commands. The more the Word requires, the better. The greater will be the quickening. What a glorious privilege it is that whenever we feel the greatest lack, we can pray to the Giver of Life. "Quicken Thou me"; give me more Life. We need quickening every day. While on earth Jesus said, "Come to me and drink." From heaven He is still saying, in the last chapter of the Bible, "Whosoever will, let him take the water of life freely." He wants to be an inexhaustible fountain of Life within us springing up and flowing out in "rivers of living water."

The repeated reading and wholehearted daily practice of this message will make the fulfillment possible. You can receive the fulfillment of any promise or requirement in the Bible. This practice is an increasing blessing to me every day, and always will be.

F. F. B.

12

God's Garden

I did the planting, Apollos did the watering, but it was God who made the seed grow. . . . you are God's field to be planted.

1 Corinthians 3:6–9 Moffatt

Every moral being on earth has been "bought with a price" to be the Lord's garden in which His "imperishable seed" is to grow and be cultivated and produce its wonders. Real Christians are God's "farm," His "husbandry," His "field," His "garden." A "field" belongs to its owner. So Paul says, "Ye are not your own; ye are bought with a price." God holds the title deed. We are absolutely His. We belong to Him by right of creation and by right of preservation. But the greatest fact is that we belong to Him by right of redemption. He "bought" us with an infinite price, to be His "field."

The Planting of the Seed

Paul said to the Corinthians, "I did the planting." In the parable of the sower, Jesus said, "The seed is the word." It is the "imperishable seed." God brings about His wonderful harvests in the same way a farmer does. Jesus said, "He sent forth a sower to sow." It is God's Word that lets us know what to trust Him for. "Faith cometh by hearing," by our knowing what God's will is for us. Because the seed can accomplish such wonders, God wants all His seed planted. God's purpose in creating seed was that it might be planted in "good ground" where it could germinate and grow and "bring forth fruit." So Paul said, "I did the planting." Seed is powerless until it is planted.

The infinite price God paid for the "field" reveals the importance of planting the "imperishable seed." All of God's wonderful works are potentially in the seed. David said, "All his work is done in faithfulness," that is, in faithfulness to His promises. God's works are prevented until the seed is in "good ground." His design for us all is that we spend our lives making possible the germination and growth of the "imperishable seed."

Nothing can take the place of the seed, not even prayer. Prayer is not the seed; the Word is the seed. The only purpose of God's promises is their fulfillment. They are all a revelation of what He is eager to do for us. The Holy Spirit, whose work it is to fulfill the promises, speaks of them as "exceeding great and precious." Their greatness is seen in their suitableness to meet all our needs and to fill all our capacities. Their immutability makes them "exceeding great and precious." They remove all reason for doubt and give us perfect reasons upon which to base our expectations. As seed, the promises cannot be changed. They therefore accomplish their wonderful results at any time and in any garden.

It is the business of Christians to prove to the world by actual demonstration that the promises of God are as true today as they were two thousand years ago. They were given to be known and recognized, claimed and pleaded in prayer.

They are to be sown and tilled by prayer. In Romans 4:12 God speaks of Christians as those "who also walk in the steps of that faith of our father Abraham." We should all treat every promise God has made to us exactly as Abraham treated God's promise to him. Can it be that God is less real to men of this Holy Spirit dispensation than He was to those who lived in the shadows of these "better things"?

Jesus said to some of the Jews in His day, "My word hath no place in you." What place should the Word of God have in us? I answer that it ought to obtain and retain a vital place in our thoughts, our memory, our conscience and our affections. It ought to obtain and retain in us a place of honor, reverence, faith, love and obedience. It ought to obtain and retain in us a place of trust. It ought to obtain and retain in us a place of authority.

Millions of people sing that glorious hymn "Standing on the Promises of God." The fact is that most of God's promises are never claimed by most modern church members. Standing on the promises of God means getting them fulfilled. It means appropriating the blessing that each promise reveals. It means praying "the prayer of faith" for their fulfillment. Neglecting the promises is equivalent to undoing what their fulfillment would mean if it were already accomplished. Their preciousness should determine our love and esteem of them. Paul was glad to say, "I did the planting." If all farmers treated their seed as millions of church members today treat God's "imperishable seed," the world would starve to death.

The Possibilities in the Seed

In the seed there are infinite possibilities. This is why it should be said of every Christian, as it was at the beginning, "They gladly received the word." In the plainest Bible text, there is a world of blessing, just as in a little seed there is a potential tree a million times bigger than the seed. One verse of Scripture allowed to germinate in a human heart may grow into a harvest of thousands of conversions and the "eternal glory" that follows. One kernel of wheat can, in time, cover a continent and feed nations. The results of cultivating the imperishable seed are as much greater and more desirable than the harvests of material seed as the heavens are higher than the earth. Only the imperishable seed can bring about imperishable results. The Bible says every seed brings forth after its kind. Each promise, by the blessing promised, reveals the nature of the fulfilled harvest.

The Watering

Paul said, "I have planted, *Apollos watered*." All the seed and all the plants in God's garden need watering. Jesus said of the stony ground on which the seed fell, "It had not much earth" (or moisture). He said, "The seed had no root." If the seed is to grow, the ground must be kept moist. It is because of the lack of constant watering that many of God's plants are withered instead of growing. A garden is a place for growth. Paul wrote to the Corinthians, "Your faith *groweth* exceedingly." Your love *groweth*. He commanded all to "grow in grace." "Therefore, God says to every one of His little gardens, 'Be filled with the Spirit.'" Keep the ground moist. The water is the Spirit "whom God hath given to them that obey Him." The fullness of the Spirit is the condition of His perfect working.

How David Watered the Seed

Every one of the 176 verses of the 119th Psalm shows David's attitude toward the Word of God. He joyfully acknowledges his obligations to keep God's precepts diligently. He promised: "I will keep thy statutes." He said to God, "Thy word have I hid in mine heart. . . . I have rejoiced in the way of thy testimonies, as much as in all riches. I will meditate in thy precepts. . . . I will delight myself in thy statutes; I will not forget thy word. . . . I have kept thy testimonies. . . . Princes also did sit and speak against me; but thy servant did meditate in thy statutes. . . . I have chosen the way of truth. . . . I will run the way of thy commandments. . . . I will observe [thy laws] with my whole heart. . . . . So shall I keep thy law continually for ever and ever. . . . I will speak of thy testimonies. . . . The proud have had me greatly in derision: yet have I not declined from thy law. . . . Thy statutes have been my songs. . . . Thou art my portion, O LORD. . . . I made haste, and delayed not to keep thy commandments. . . . The proud have forged a lie against me: but I will keep thy precepts with my whole heart. . . . I delight in Thy law. . . . The law of thy mouth is better unto me than thousands of gold and silver. . . . For ever, O LORD, thy word is settled in heaven. Thy faithfulness is unto all generations. . . . Unless thy law had been my delight, I should then have perished in mine affliction. I will never forget thy precepts. . . . O how love I thy law! it is my meditation all the day. . . . I have refrained my feet from every evil way, that I might keep thy word. . . . How sweet are thy words unto my taste! yea, sweeter than honey to my mouth! . . . Thy word is a lamp unto my feet, and a light unto my path. I have sworn, and I will perform it, that I will keep thy righteous judgments. . . . Thy testimonies have I taken as an heritage for ever: for they are the rejoicing of my heart. I have inclined my heart to perform thy statutes alway, even unto the end. I hate vain thoughts; but thy law do I love. . . . I will have respect unto thy statutes continually. . . . I love thy commandments above gold; yea, above fine gold. . . . I esteem all thy precepts concerning all things to be right; and I hate every false way. Thy testimonies are wonderful: therefore doth my soul keep them. . . . Many are my persecutors and mine enemies; yet do I not decline from thy testimonies. . . . My heart standeth in awe of thy word. I rejoice at thy word, as one that findeth great spoil."

All of these statements, and many more, are in this 119ᵗʰ Psalm. They show us how David watered the Word. Paul said the one who plants and the one who waters are equal. *Watering* the seed is as necessary as *planting* it. God won't make the seed grow unless we water it.

God Makes the Seed Grow

And then Paul said, it is "God that giveth the increase." He made His promises for this one purpose. He *always* makes the seed grow when it is kept in good ground and *watered*. The *growing* comes after the *watering*.

Jesus also said, "It bringeth forth much fruit." The seed *always* brings forth fruit. The intensity of all holy desire is measured by the degree of divine love that one possesses. *God's* desire, therefore, is as much greater than ours as His love is greater than ours. His benevolence is so great that His eyes "run to and fro throughout the whole earth" continually seeking opportunities to bless those whose attitude of heart makes it possible. What God has promised *belongs* to us. The justice of God requires that He make the seed grow when it is planted and watered. John says, "He is faithful and just." The word *just* means God would be unjust to withhold from us what He promises. We have a *right* to what He promises us. It is a 100 percent fact that God makes every seed grow when it is planted and watered. We can all prove this to our present and eternal delight. God is the best farmer in the universe. He never fails!

God's Time Is Now

The work of the "imperishable seed" is *supernatural*, because it is God alone who makes the seed grow. Seeds often produce their wonderful results the same day they are planted. God's promises are for *today*; His *time* is always *today*. "*Today* if ye will hear his voice, harden not your hearts" (Hebrews 4:7). If you delay the acceptance of God's promises, you may not be alive tomorrow. The promises of God belong to us *today*, and we are not sure of them any other time. The only way to be sure of God's promised blessings is to accept *His time*; and we read in 2 Corinthians 6:2, "Behold, *now* is the accepted time." Since *now* is the time God accepts, we should accept it as *our* time. He commands us to hear His voice "*today*," and says "Harden not your hearts" by waiting. In Mark 11:24, Jesus said "Believe that ye receive" (literally "*take*"). *When*? "*Now*," "when ye pray." Faith says, before the answer is manifested, "Father, I thank Thee that Thou hast heard me." When you cannot *see* or *feel*, say, "This is the time to trust." The results are not to be manifested until after we believe our prayer is heard and continue to believe. Say to God: "Thou art now working in response to my faith; I count on Thy faithfulness." The matter passes out of our hands into God's hands the moment we make a definite committal of it to God. Paul said, "He is able to keep that which *I have committed* unto Him." But God does not promise to keep anything that is not committed to Him.

This is the way to receive everything God has promised to us. Were the gifts of God for soul and body merely *promised* gifts, we would have to wait for the Promiser to fulfill

His promises. The responsibility would be on Him. But all of God's blessings are *offered* gifts as well as promised, and therefore need to be *accepted*. The responsibility for their transfer is *ours*. This clears God of all responsibility for any failure.

The Effect of Watering the Seed

What was the effect of David's attitude toward God's Word, of his watering the seed? This shepherd boy, by watering the Word within him, became wiser than all his teachers. His attitude toward God's Word made him "a man after God's own heart." It made him the world's greatest psalmist. His psalms have blessed millions during the centuries that have followed. His watering of the seed made him a divinely inspired writer. As every seed planted, in turn, produces *more seed*, so David's words in the Psalms became God's imperishable seed, which have for centuries germinated in human hearts all over the world. His words have been the texts for thousands of sermons.

David found that meditation chews our spiritual food and gets the sweetness. It extracts the nutritive virtue of the Word into our hearts and lives. Meditation has a digesting power and turns truth into spiritual nourishment. It is the Word of God that Paul says "effectually worketh" in us all the divine transformations from "glory to glory." David said, "I understand more than the ancients because I keep Thy precepts." By observing in his heart and life the precepts of the Lord, David understood, early in life, more than those who lived in earlier times. He knew more than they learned in a whole lifetime by experience. David, who started life only as a shepherd boy, by meditating in and practicing divine precepts, obtained such wisdom and knowledge that he was spoken of in 2 Samuel 14:17 as "an angel of God." He was able to judge right and wrong. In the same chapter, his wisdom is compared to "the wisdom of an angel." He said, "Thy word hath quickened me." It quickened his whole being to the extent that God's Word was fulfilled in him. His life was filled with praise and thanksgiving. How much better to be the Lord's garden than the devil's! The possibilities of the "imperishable seed" are infinite. Nothing can be so beneficial as being God's garden. Only God can know what the eternal harvest will be. Remember that throughout your Christian life, *you are God's field to be planted.*

13

Why Some Fail to Receive Healing from Christ

Twenty-two Reasons for Failure to Be Healed

It is so clearly revealed throughout the Scriptures that the heavenly Father wills our healing. Why do some who seek healing fail to receive it? This question is in the minds of many honest inquirers. There are several answers to this question, which we will mention briefly. By these answers many have been helped who had previously failed to receive healing. Consequently, they have been gloriously healed.

1. Insufficient Instruction

The first reason for not receiving healing is ignorance concerning the healing power of the Gospel. Paul tells us that "faith cometh by hearing, and hearing by the word of God." Many have sought healing from Christ before they heard or knew enough of the Word of God. They have not had a steadfast faith. Those in the early Church were in one accord in the matter of proclaiming all the Gospel. They kept back nothing that was profitable. Paul declared "all the counsel of God."

We have seen that God's way of producing *faith for healing* is the same as that of producing *faith for salvation*. This is the way for any other blessing. The needy one should first learn, from the Scriptures, what God's will is in the matter. The hand of faith cannot reach out and take from God what the eye of faith does not first see to be the will of God. Jesus said, "Ye shall know the truth, and the truth shall make you free." It is the truth of the written Word that sets us free. Freedom is the truth known, understood, received, acted on, maintained and steadfastly believed with an appropriating faith.

Paul tells us that it is "the Word of God, which effectually worketh in [them] that believe." The Word of God is the "precious seed"; the "imperishable seed." It is the seed that has the power. It never fails to do its own work. It must be *known* and *received* and *kept* in "the good ground," the only place the good seed can grow.

Some fail to receive healing because they are trying to get results from the seed, the Word concerning healing, without knowing what that Word is. They try to get results without giving the Word its place, without keeping the good seed in "the good ground." The seed cannot work in us unless it *is in us by our having known and received it.*

God said, "I am the Lord that healeth thee," and promised to take away all our sicknesses. But He *first* said, "If thou wilt diligently hearken . . . and do all." This means to be diligent in the matter of knowing, understanding and practicing what God says in His Word on the subject of healing. *We must know what God offers to us before we can expect to receive it from Him. The knowledge of God's will must precede faith for His will to be done.* Multitudes today do not know that the perfect healing of their bodies is the fully revealed will of God in His written Word, the Bible. To know this, is the *only sufficient evidence for appropriating faith.*

Those seeking healing can say when tested, "It is written." They can then quote God's promises to Satan. This settles the question of God's will. Without this, their faith cannot remain steadfast. Many sufferers have prayed for healing for years without success. This is because they have prayed *the faith-destroying phrase*, "If it be Thy will." Then later, they have been healed through the truth of God's Word contained and explained in this book.

The early Church was in one accord in teaching this truth. The believers also lifted up their voices to God in one accord in prayer for "signs and wonders" of healing. They prayed "the prayer of faith" before the sick were brought into the streets of Jerusalem. It was not the faith of *a single evangelist*, but the faith of *the entire company of believers*. This brought healing to *everyone* in the streets of Jerusalem after Christ's ascension (Acts 5:14–16).

The majority of ministers and Christians today are bound by their traditions of ultradispensationalism on the subject of the ministry of healing. Through their lack of understanding the Word, they are opposed to it as it was taught, preached and practiced in the early Church.

Church members, as a whole, have not accepted our Lord's attitude toward sickness as revealed in the gospels. They cannot pray with one accord for these healing results as the early Church did. In our day, opposition often takes the place of united prayer. Unbelief takes the place of united faith. Unlike the early Church, lukewarmness takes the place of being Spirit-filled. I will ask *you* the question. Since we are members one of another, may not the blame for the failure of some to receive healing today be largely due to the unbelieving part of the Church itself? I believe you will agree to this.

We so often hear it said "the day of miracles has passed." Suppose it were generally believed that the day of regeneration has passed. How this would hinder the work of the ministry in that part of the Gospel! Christian workers could have no success in saving souls. They would have to first get people to give up the false tradition and put the Word of God in its place. On the other hand, suppose that from infancy we had all been taught the healing part of the Gospel. In this case, I am sure, very few would have any difficulty in evidencing faith for healing.

It is the Word of God that produces faith for healing. We have had the joy of seeing hundreds healed while they were listening to the truth on that subject. Others have been healed while reading our printed instructions. These answered their questions and removed the hindrances to their faith.

2. Lack of United Prayer

The second reason why some fail to receive healing is an enlargement on what we have already said. Christ planned to continue His healing ministry during His absence. This was to be accomplished by His whole Church, which is His Body, not through an obscure member of that Body. He said, "These signs shall follow *them*," *the Church*, not "him," the individual. Christ had gone away, and had sent His successor, the Holy Spirit. It was not the faith of a lone or solitary evangelist but that of a Spirit-filled Church. This brought healing to all the sick in the streets of Jerusalem.

Today some do not like public healing services. When God had His way, He had the multitudes healed right on the streets. He wanted His compassion to be made known to the world as a basis for faith. God began His works in this dispensation as He wants them continued, through the whole Church. Every member should be *filled* and *kept filled* with the Holy Spirit.

The greatest number of conversions today are brought about by an outpouring of the Holy Spirit and through a Church that is in one accord. This is the way that all were healed in the streets of Jerusalem.

Most of God's dealings with men, both in saving and healing, are by the outpouring of His Spirit and through a Spirit-filled, united and praying Church. His method is revealed by the promise, "I will pour out my Spirit," and the statement, "They were all filled with the Spirit." A Spirit-filled and praying Church produces an atmosphere in which it is easy for God to work. This makes it difficult for the devil to interfere. *This atmosphere is the Holy Spirit Himself.* He is more than a match for the devil.

In the revival belt, during the Finney revivals and other great revivals, sinners fell under conviction as soon as they stepped off the train where a revival was in progress. Mr. Finney tells of such a unity in prayer that every adult person on a street three miles long was saved, except one. The Christians unitedly prayed for that one, and he was saved.

It is true that individuals are sometimes saved and healed where there is no revival. However, God's *regular* way is for His people all to pray for an outpouring of the Holy Spirit. We read, "These all continued with one accord in prayer and supplication." We seldom see such a thing now! Some of our theology today causes many people to anchor in past blessings. They do not have a daily renewing of the fullness that constituted the initial blessing. Then Christians were filled with the Spirit. Unless the Church is filled and kept filled with the Holy Spirit it is impossible that the spiritual atmosphere of the meetings can be what it must be. Otherwise, God is limited or hindered. This atmosphere is produced by the whole Church being filled with the Spirit and all praying for the work of Christ. Then the power of God is present to heal as it was at the beginning. God's way is for the whole Church to be filled and kept filled with the same Holy Spirit who saved and healed those multitudes in New Testament times.

The results of the fulfillment of divine promises are the same in any age. If you want to know how the Spirit acts now, just read how He *acted* when He had full possession of the Church. The book of Acts is a blueprint by which the Holy Spirit wishes to work throughout His dispensation. The early Christians in Acts 4 were all filled with the Spirit; all prevailed in prayer for "signs and wonders" of healing. In James 5 all Christians are commanded to pray for the healing of the sick, and to do it as earnestly as Elijah prayed for rain. When this was done in the early Church, "the prayer of faith" by the *elders* was but voicing the prayer of the whole Church.

John says, "This is the confidence that we have in him, that, if we ask anything according to his will, he heareth us." This was proven by the whole company of Christians in the fourth chapter of the Acts. *Every Christian today is commanded to be filled with the Spirit, to pray for the outpouring of the Spirit and to prevail in prayer for the healing of the sick.* Every priest should be exercising his priesthood. The failure of the majority to do this in our day pollutes the atmosphere of the meetings. It makes it harder for the sick to have faith and for the Holy Spirit to work.

The failure of Christians to live and walk in the Spirit limits the Holy One of Israel. *Our being filled with the Spirit is the condition for His perfect working.* Instead of being surrounded by this atmosphere in our day, a poor, afflicted wife often is surrounded with opposition from her own family. Sometimes she gets opposition from her own pastor and fellow church members. She fails to receive healing, being too weak in mind and body to fight the battle alone. The very ones who are opposing her are the ones who ought to be praying in faith for her healing. We are *all* to "bear one another's burdens, and so fulfill the law of Christ."

Those in the early Church met the condition of being filled with the Spirit. Today it is the very ones who are violating these conditions who are asking why some fail to receive healing. The answer is because these very doubters are making it impossible for the Church to be in one accord in prayer and faith for the sick. The Church is out of tune with God's program.

A remarkable document is signed by twenty bishops of the Episcopal Church in the Commonwealth of Australia. It gives a wonderful report of the miracles of healing manifested in the cathedrals of that Church in the various cities of that country. In this report they say:

> The faith which is needed is not merely individual but corporate faith, the faith of the home, of the ministry and of the whole Church. The Body, not a lone member of it, must cooperate with Christ its Head if its sick members are all to be healed. The most marked groups after the mission, came from parishes where the wave of intercession had been highest and swept farthest. . . . The world today is waiting for a fresh revelation of the presence and Power of God in the work of the Church and in the life of its members. It has already seen and felt once more the wonder of Divine healing.

Today a large part of the members of the Church, through ignorance, are opposing that for which the early Church prevailed in prayer. They have not accepted our Lord's attitude toward sickness. They have not met the conditions for the healing of the sick that God desires. It is these very hinderers who are pointing out the failures for which they themselves are largely responsible.

It is not uncommon today to find those, who ought to be doing the works of Christ, warning the sick to stay away from places where the works of Christ are being done. Would it not be better for them to warn the people against going where confirmation or baptism or church membership or reformation are put in the place of the new birth?

3. Community Unbelief

The third reason why some fail to receive healing from Christ is community unbelief. Jesus worked miracles and healed all that were sick. When He came to His hometown of Nazareth where He had been brought up, "He could not do any miracles there . . . [because of] their unbelief" (Mark 6:5–6 Weymouth). Think of it! Christ Himself, under the full anointing of the Holy Ghost, was *hindered by community unbelief.* Since this is true, is it strange that today some in any city should fail to receive healing? In Nazareth God would not allow the gift of miracles to operate through Christ where, by their unbelief, the people were making Him a liar. Why should He do so today? Paul had better success in working miracles among the heathen than Jesus had in His hometown (Acts 14).

On the subject of healing, people have been taught today to believe in traditions in the place of the plain Word of God. This has turned the whole world into a veritable Nazareth of unbelief. I mean by that, today community unbelief is almost general. Those who preach the full Gospel and pray for the sick are obliged to labor in a Nazareth of unbelief. We can get only as far as we can get rid of the "traditions of men" regarding healing. We have to teach the people what the Scriptures actually teach on the subject. By doing this, I boldly say that Jesus Christ (not ourselves) has had greater success in working miracles in all the cities where our revival campaigns have been conducted than He had in Nazareth, His own hometown. Now, don't misquote me. I am not saying that *we* have had success. I am talking about what Christ has done. Whenever and wherever the people have been enlightened by our ministry, they know their privilege in the matter of healing.

The fact that Christ could do no miracle in Nazareth only proved the unbelief of the people. If, as some are teaching, the sick are to be healed *without their faith*, why didn't Jesus go ahead and heal the sick in Nazareth? The Bible answers, "because of *their* unbelief."

Some Christians today explain the failure of some to receive healing by calling in question Christ's willingness to heal all sick persons. They should then call in question His willingness to save all sinners, in order to explain the fact that so many in the churches are unsaved.

Upon a certain occasion only one woman in a great throng touched Jesus with faith for healing. Later on, whole multitudes did so. It is a matter of enlightenment and faith.

The nine disciples had failed to deliver the epileptic boy mentioned in the gospels. Some theologian of that day, if he were like many of the theologians of these days, might have seized upon that failure. He might say, "There, now we have the proof that it is not always God's will to heal." But the father wanted the boy to be healed. The boy himself wanted to be healed. The disciples, divinely commissioned to cast out devils and heal the sick, wanted him to be healed. Under similar circumstances today someone would say because of such a failure, "It is not God's will that such an one should be healed." They would make theology out of the failure. But Jesus came down from the mountain and delivered the boy. This proves it to be God's will to heal, even when His accredited representatives had failed to heal. *Why not make theology out of this?*

When the father of this boy said to Jesus, "If Thou canst do anything," Jesus refused to take the responsibility for any failure. He said, "If thou canst believe. . . ." Then the father cried out, "Lord, I believe; help thou mine unbelief." Of course, he received the help asked for. He succeeded where the apostles had failed. Christ delivered the boy.

The fact is that in the healing ministry we are compelled to labor in the face of almost universal unbelief. Those who preach only the salvation of the soul part of the Gospel are laboring in the midst of the almost universal acceptance of that doctrine. However, God is giving proofs of divine healing as bright and as convincing as the proofs of regeneration. This is with not nearly so much teaching to produce faith. When I think of the lack of teaching on divine healing, and the unspiritual condition of the churches, I am not surprised at the lack of faith, because of their general attitude toward this part of forgotten orthodoxy. Instead of wondering why some are not healed, I marvel at the success God is giving to those who pray for the sick. I have seen many deaf mutes healed when scarcely a person in the audience expected the healing.

Thousands now testify that they have been divinely healed and are in good health physically. The general average of professing Christians in any church is not always spiritually healthy. Would not the *physical* health of those who testify that they have been divinely healed compare favorably with the *spiritual* health of those who oppose the Gospel of healing? Is the average professed Christian any better proof of the doctrine of regeneration than those who testify to having been divinely *healed* are of the doctrine of divine healing? They ought to be, because they have heard that part of the Word of God all their lives. The majority of those who are healed when we pray for them, have heard the plain teaching of the Word of God concerning divine healing for only a few days. There are many today who have been divinely healed after having been deaf and dumb from birth. They can hear better *physically* than the average church member can hear *spiritually*. I have seen many who could not walk a step until after they had been prayed for, who are now walking better *physically* than the average Christian is walking *spiritually*. The average Christian, all of his life, has heard the Word of God, which teaches the healing of the *soul*, whereas these others have heard only a few times the Word of God, which teaches the healing of the *body*.

Are all who have been baptized washed from all their sins? No, but those who have faith are. What water is in the ordinance of Christian baptism, oil is in the ordinance of anointing the sick for healing.

Suppose someone should say to me, "So-and-so was anointed but was not healed." I would answer, "So-and-so was baptized but was not saved and was not healed from the disease of sin." If a man should say to me, "I know a man whom you anointed whose body was not healed," I would say to him, "I know a man whom you baptized whose soul was not healed." Thousands who have been baptized have never been regenerated. This is infinitely worse than for a Christian to fail to receive healing for his body.

Some say, "If so-and-so should be healed, I will believe in divine healing." Why not be consistent? Say, "If so-and-so should get saved, I will believe in salvation." This is the same as to say, "I will believe so-and-so's experience in preference to God, the Bible and the experiences of all the other thousands who have been saved and healed." After God has healed thousands from all their afflictions, why not say to Him, "I will not believe unless You heal one more."

185

Would you reject the doctrine of consecration because some church members are not consecrated, while thousands of others are? I heard a minister say, concerning the work of another evangelist, "So-and-so was anointed and prayed for, but died without being healed." Yet this same minister baptized so-and-so and took him into the Church, thereby proclaiming to the world that his soul had been healed from the disease of sin. But the man died without the new birth, and his soul was lost. This is infinitely worse than for a sick Christian to fail to be healed and to die and wake up in glory.

Suppose the testimony of those of us who say we have been healed is rejected, because after a careful examination by a medical expert, it could be shown that we fall short of physical perfection. To be consistent, why should we not have a spiritual expert with spiritual discernment, such as the apostle Paul had, examine those in the modern Church who oppose the Gospel of healing. Let him reject the testimony of all those among them who do not measure up spiritually to what the Bible represents a healthy soul to be.

After witnessing the miraculous healing of thousands, I am convinced that the proofs of healing are as bright and convincing as are the proofs of regeneration. Yet I do not base any doctrine on these answers to prayer. I, for one, will preach all the Gospel if I never see another man saved or healed as long as I live. I am determined to base my doctrines on the immutable Word of God, not on phenomena or human experience.

No minister can get results until, by preaching the Word of God, he can produce faith for what that Word offers. Sixty thousand churches in the United States reported no conversions in a whole year. However, I am not going to offer this fact as a reason for fighting the doctrine of regeneration, or any other part of the Gospel.

Some say, "We believe in healing, but we do not believe in parading it." I have noticed that some who fail to rejoice with those who succeed in receiving healing from Christ are quick to parade a failure. They say nothing about the successes. To me it is a mystery how any Christian can fail to rejoice when a poor afflicted person has been healed by Christ. I not only rejoice when a sufferer has been healed by Christ, but I am glad to parade God's mercy to the world. "Make known His deeds among the people" is the command of God. Jesus commanded the demoniac, out of whom He cast the devil, to go back to his own community and tell what great mercy Christ had shown him. The Scriptures tell us that he published throughout Decapolis this mercy of Christ. In the next chapter we read of multitudes in Decapolis being healed by Christ. The multitudes glorified the God of Israel.

4. The Traditions of Men

The healing part of the Gospel is hindered and even made void by the traditions of men. Jesus said to the Jewish teachers of His day, "Why do ye also transgress the commandment of God by your tradition?" In our day most preachers have done worse. They have made void a part of the Gospel by their traditions.

• One tradition is *that God is the author of disease* and that He wills the sickness of some of His worshipers. It is a mystery to me how anyone can hold this view in the face of the Scriptures and the ministry of Christ. For three years Jesus healed all that were oppressed by the devil, or at least all that came to Him for healing.

If sickness is the will of God for His worshipers, then every physician is a lawbreaker, every trained nurse is defying the Almighty and every hospital is a house of rebellion instead of a house of mercy. If God wants one to be sick, it is a sin for that one even to want to be well, because we are to love the will of God, whatever that will may be.

• Another tradition that is responsible for thousands dying a premature death after years of physical agony is the teaching that *we can glorify God more by remaining sick and exhibiting patience than we can by being divinely healed.* An honest but unenlightened minister will often kneel at the bedside of one suffering with arthritis or cancer or some other dangerous disease. He prays, "Lord, since in Thy loving providence Thou hast seen fit to lay Thine afflicting hand upon our dear sister, give her fortitude and patience to bear this affliction." He does this instead of obeying the plain command to anoint "any sick" in the Church and to pray "the prayer of faith" for their healing (James 5:14–15). John Wesley said this method was the only process of healing in the Church until it was lost through unbelief.

Many are taught that one can glorify God more by remaining sick than by being healed. If this is true, then Jesus did not hesitate to rob His Father of all the glory He possibly could. He healed everyone who appealed to Him for help during His entire earthly ministry. His Successor, the Holy Spirit, was sent down to augment what Christ had begun to do and to teach. He did not hesitate to rob God of all the glory He could by healing everyone in the streets of Jerusalem (Acts 5:15–16). Paul did not hesitate to rob God of all the glory he could by healing all the other sick on the island of Melita.

• The most common and threadbare tradition is the worn-out statement, *"The age of miracles has passed."* Of all the present-day traditions of the elders or ministers, this is the most foolish, illogical and unscriptural of any that I know.

The Holy Spirit, in whose age we are now living, is God's only Miracle-Worker, the only administrator of the Father's will. He is the One who healed all the sick multitudes who came to Christ for healing during the days of His flesh. All the miracles ever wrought until the Day of Pentecost were accomplished by the Spirit, the Miracle-Worker. This was before He had entered officially into His own dispensation.

The age in which we live was intended by our heavenly Father to be the most miraculous of all the dispensations. It is the Miracle-Worker's age; the Holy Spirit's dispensation. During this age the great promise is that God will pour out the Holy Spirit, the Miracle-Worker, upon all flesh. This is the only age in which the Miracle-Worker would incarnate Himself in us. This is the only age in which the nine gifts of the Spirit, including the gifts of faith, healing and miracles, were to be distributed to every man severally as He, the Holy Spirit, will. Jesus declared that the works that He was doing would be continued and that even "greater works" would be done by the Holy Spirit, the Miracle-Worker. This was after He entered office during Christ's exaltation. This is the Spirit's dispensation.

How absurd and ridiculous for any professed Bible teacher to pick out this, the Miracle-Worker's age, as the only age when miracles are not to be done! How absurd for such a one to teach that the Holy Spirit will work miracles in every age but His own age! This is a "better" dispensation, with a "better" Priest, "better" covenant . . . better" promises, and "better" everything than any previous age.

Some talk as though the present age is not the Holy Spirit's age. There is but one dispensation of the Holy Spirit, and that one lies between the first and second advents of our Lord. It is true, we are living in the Laodicean or lukewarm period of the Spirit's dispensation. At the beginning of the age the

Church was in her Spirit-filled period, and we are now in the lukewarm period of the same age. But, for one (and, thank God! there are many others like me), I am going to base both my preaching and my practicing on the preaching and the practicing of the Church during her Spirit-filled period. This is better than operating on the preaching and practicing of the Church during her lukewarm period. I would rather labor to lift the true Church up to the Bible standard of the first century than to try to make the Bible fit the standard of the lukewarm Church of the twentieth century. In previous discourses we have seen that God has worked miracles in each of the centuries since the closing of the Scriptures, down to our day. This worn-out tradition that we are considering is entirely set aside by the facts of history.

• Another tradition is that *it is not God's will to heal all.* In previous chapters we have answered this objection from every conceivable angle. If it is God's will to heal only some of those who need healing, then none have any basis for faith, until they shall have received a special revelation that they are among the favored ones. If God's promises to heal are not for all, then no man can ascertain the will of God for himself from the Bible. Are we to understand from such teachers that we must close our Bibles and get our revelation directly from the Spirit before we can pray for the sick? Cannot the will of God in this matter be ascertained from the Scriptures? This would be virtually to teach that the whole of the divine activity on the line of healing would have to be governed by direct revelations from the Spirit instead of by the Scriptures.

• Still others are hindered from receiving healing by being taught to add to their prayer for healing the faith-destroying phrase, *"If it be Thy will."* There is only one case given in the New Testament of one asking for healing in this way. That is the case of the leper, who said, "If thou wilt, thou canst make me whole." This man could not have prayed otherwise because he was not yet informed as to the will of God in the matter. Jesus did not heal this leper until He had added to his faith the fact that Jesus *could* heal him, then the faith that Jesus *would* heal him. The "I will" of Jesus canceled the "if" of the leper. It is impossible for one ever to pray with faith until the "if" has been removed from his prayer. To have real faith is to be "fully persuaded" that God will do what He has promised to do. No one is ever "fully persuaded" when he adds to his prayer, "If it be Thy will." Since God has revealed His will in this matter by His promises, for us to say, "If it be Thy will," when praying for healing is the same as to say, "If it be Thy will to keep Thy promise."

• Another unscriptural premise, which has sent thousands of sufferers to premature graves and kept multitudes of others from receiving healing, is the modern teaching that *Paul's thorn in the flesh* was some kind of physical trouble. The falsity of this position is shown in the following chapter, "Paul's Thorn."

The expression "thorn in the flesh" is not once used in either the Old or the New Testament except as an illustration. The figure of the "thorn in the flesh" is not in one single instance used in the Bible as a figure of sickness. Every time the phrase is used in the Bible it is specifically stated exactly what the "thorn in the flesh" was. For instance, in Numbers 33:55 Moses spoke to the children of Israel, before they entered the land of Canaan. He said, "If ye will not drive out the inhabitants of the land from before you; then it shall come to pass, that those which ye let remain of them shall be pricks in your eyes, and thorns in your sides, and shall vex ye in the land wherein ye dwell."

Here the Scripture itself plainly tells us what the "pricks" in the eyes and the "thorns" in the sides of the Israelites were. They were the inhabitants of Canaan that had been spared, not eye trouble or sickness. God was only using this as an illustration to show that as a thorn sticking in the flesh is annoying, so the Canaanites, if allowed to remain in the land, would be a constant annoyance to the children of Israel. In all the other places in the Bible where this expression is used, the thorns are personalities.

In each of the other instances the Bible definitely states what the thorn was. In this particular instance Paul definitely states what his thorn was. He said it was "The messenger [Greek *angelos*] of Satan," or, as translated by others, "the angel of the devil," "Satan's angel," etc.

The Greek word *angelos* appears 188 times in the Bible. It is translated "angel" 181 times and "messenger" the other 7 times. In every one of the 188 times where this word is used in the Bible, it means a person, not a thing. Hell was made for "the devil and his angels." An angel or a messenger is always a person that one person sends to another, never a disease.

Paul not only tells us that his thorn was an angel, or messenger of Satan, but he also tells us what that angel came to do. He said that he was sent "to buffet me," in the same way "the waves buffeted" the boat, and the soldiers "buffeted" Christ. Weymouth translates this passage in this way, "Satan's angel dealing blow after blow." *Buffeting* means giving *repeated* blows. If Paul's buffeting was a physical one, it would have had to be a succession of diseases, or the same disease repeated many times. Otherwise, he could not have termed it *buffeting.*

In speaking of this messenger or angel, Rotherham's translation uses the personal pronoun *he.* Weymouth's translation says, "As to this, three times I besought the

Lord to rid me of *him*." These two pronouns, as well as the word *angel* or *messenger*, prove what Paul's thorn was. He himself plainly shows that it was a satanic personality, not a disease. Paul could not have used the personal pronouns *he* and *him* when speaking of a disease, because there is no personality to disease. Paul enumerates almost every kind of trouble one can think of as his buffeting, but disease is not on the list.

Jesus revealed to us the unchanging will of God by what He did. He healed every sick person that ever applied to Him for healing, but He did not promise to take away the buffetings or persecution. Paul was the most prolific teacher in the Bible on the subject of divine healing.

• Another tradition that has hindered the ministry of healing is the teaching that *Jesus healed the sick as the Son of God, not as the Son of Man*. Such teachers believe that as we are not Christ, we cannot expect such works today. The Scriptures teach us that Jesus, the Son of God, emptied Himself and became like unto His brethren in all things, except as to sin. He speaks of Himself as "the Son of man" about eighty times. As the Son of Man He said, "I can of mine own self do nothing." This certainly was not true of Him before He became the Son of Man. All things were made by Him and for Him. We have already seen that Jesus did His works in reliance on the Spirit. He "began both to do and teach, until the day He was taken up," what He Himself promised in John 14:12. These things He would continue and augment in answer to the prayers of the Church when He was glorified. The very words here quoted from Acts 1:1, "Jesus *began* both to do and teach," prove that what the Lord "began" both in *doing and teaching* was to be continued by the Holy Spirit operating through the Church.

5. Breaking Natural Laws

The failure of some to receive healing is because of the breaking of natural laws. Let it be remembered that natural laws are God's laws and that they are as divine as are His miracles. Nature is God in action, but not miraculously. Because of their ignorance of natural laws some are not supplying their bodies with the required nourishment, or they may be overeating, while asking God to heal them of stomach trouble, and thereby hindering the answer to their prayers. After God had revealed Himself as Jehovah-Rapha, our Healer, the conditions He imposed were that the people observe His laws of health. There are times when sufferers who are ignorant of dietetics and other simple requirements need the advice of someone who is qualified to give advice in such matters.

6. Unbelief of Elder or Minister Who Prays

Some are not healed because of unbelief on the part of the elder or minister who prays for them. Christ's disciples, although divinely commissioned to cast out devils and to heal the sick, failed to deliver the epileptic boy. When Jesus came down from the mountain He delivered the boy and rebuked the disciples for their unbelief.

7. An Evil Spirit Must Be Cast Out

Some are not healed because their affliction is the work of an evil spirit that must be cast out. Jesus did not heal the epileptic *disease* but cast out the epileptic *spirit*. He also cast out the deaf and dumb and blind spirits. He says of those who believe, "In my name they shall cast out demons." Many times we have seen people instantly delivered when we rebuked the afflicting spirit. We spoke representatively, in Christ's name, or by His authority.

194

8. The Sick Person's Sin

Some fail to receive healing because they regard iniquity in their heart. These should learn to say with David: "If I regard iniquity in my heart, the Lord will not hear me." God has not promised to destroy the works of the devil in the body while we are clinging to the works of the devil in the soul. Unconfessed sin hinders people from receiving God's mercy. His Word tells us, "He that covereth his sins shall not prosper: but whoso confesseth and forsaketh them shall have mercy."

9. Lukewarmness of the Church

In this Laodicean period of the Church, lukewarmness is one of the great hindrances to healing. After Christ was glorified, He sent down the message, "I would thou wert cold or hot. So then because thou art lukewarm, and neither cold nor hot, I will spew thee out of my mouth."

The best thing for us is to be red hot for God. The next best thing is to be cold. But, it is fatal to be lukewarm, for the Lord said He would spew out the lukewarm.

Lukewarmness is a much worse disease than cancer; therefore God wants to heal lukewarmness first. He has promised and is waiting to heal our backsliding and flood our hearts with His love. God says of the man whose heart is hot with love for Him, "Because he hath set his love upon me, therefore will I deliver him." Serving God with gladness and cheerfulness of heart was the condition for healing in Old Testament times. Surely the standard ought not be lowered in this day of grace!

10. Unwillingness to Surrender to God

Some fail to receive healing because sickness and affliction are the natural result of a heart that is not willing to follow

God into the center of His will. When man surrenders his will to his loving Father, healing follows. It is God's will that we learn the pleasure of serving Him and living out His divine program for our lives. It is impossible to pray "the prayer of faith" for those who are unwilling to be led into the glorious center of God's will.

11. An Unforgiving Spirit

An unforgiving spirit, or holding a grudge, hinders some from receiving the Lord's healing. Jesus said, "If ye forgive not men their trespasses, neither will your heavenly Father forgive your trespasses." The first thing we need and the first thing God wants to grant us is the forgiveness of our sins, but God cannot forgive us when we will not forgive others. If He cannot forgive us, He certainly cannot heal us. Many times we have seen the afflicted healed "in the twinkling of an eye" when they were ready to forgive those who had wronged them.

12. A Need to Seek Forgiveness

Wrongs that have not been made right hinder the faith of some to receive healing. Those who have wronged their neighbor in any way must ask his forgiveness. We have known many who, terribly afflicted, were healed as soon as this was done.

13. Lack of Diligence

Some have no diligence when seeking God for healing. God "is a rewarder of them that diligently seek Him." We have known sufferers to undergo as many as a dozen or more operations without any positive promise of being healed. Yet in coming to God for healing, which He positively promises to give, many do not come with anything like the diligence shown by those who apply for help from man.

14. Seeking Miracles, Not Healing

Because of improper instruction, many fail to be healed because they endeavor to confine God to miracles. Because they are not made well and strong in an instant, these people cast away their confidence.

God differentiates between a miracle and a healing. If every man, wasted with disease, were made strong and well in a moment, there would be no healings. They would all be miracles. When enumerating the spiritual gifts, Paul speaks of gifts of healing and also of miracles. Christ could do no miracle in Nazareth because of the unbelief of the people, but He did heal a few sick folk there. Confusing healings with miracles is a very common hindrance to healing in these days, when there is so little clear teaching on the subject.

15. Watching Symptoms

Some weaken their faith by watching their symptoms. Instead of doing this, they should become strong in faith, like Abraham of old, by looking unto the promise of God. God has made His Word the only basis for faith. Some people defeat their own healing by making their feelings the basis for faith.

16. Failure to Act on Faith

Others fail to receive healing because they do not act their faith. "Faith without works is dead." It is not God's turn to move until we have faith with corresponding actions. The literal translation of Mark 11:22, "Have faith in God," is *"Reckon on God's faithfulness."*

The full exercise of faith means that we *think* faith, *speak* faith, *act* faith. To the blind man, Jesus said, "Go, wash in the Pool of Siloam." This act gave the man an opportunity to exercise faith in heart, mind and body. He was not healed

197

until he had first given this visible expression of his faith. He believed the healing was his *before* it was manifested.

It was the same with Naaman, the leper, and also with the ten lepers. Jesus said, "Go, shew yourselves to the priests." The record is, "As they went, they were cleansed." *A visible expression* of faith, including their heart, mind and body, was required *before* their healing was manifested. Some miss being healed by reversing this divine order.

17. Lack of Confidence

Others, when tested, cast away their confidence. They fail to see that, as with Abraham, their faith should be perfected by the test, not destroyed.

We are made partakers of God's promises on the condition that we hold the beginning of our confidence steady until the promises are fulfilled (Hebrews 10:35). If the Word of God is the reason for our faith, then it is never right to cast away our confidence in it.

18. Not Receiving the Holy Spirit

Some fail to receive healing by neglecting to receive the Holy Spirit. He was sent to impart to us the blessings of redemption. In Romans 8:11 Paul tells us that our mortal (not actually but judicially dead) bodies (also) are to be given life by the Spirit that dwells *in* (not outside of) us. Since our bodies are the temples of the Holy Ghost, and the Holy Ghost applies the healing, we might say that He is the Carpenter who repairs the house. Some are consciously keeping the Carpenter outside of the house while asking Him to repair it on the inside. Paul said, "The body for the Lord" before he said, "The Lord for the body." We must present our bodies a living sacrifice (Romans 12:1) and let them become the temples of the Holy Ghost if we want them healed. This reason for failure does not usually apply to those who are untaught as to their privilege of being filled with the Spirit.

19. Lack of Faith

Some are not healed because they substitute their belief in the doctrine of divine healing for personal faith to be healed.

20. Failure to Receive God's Promises

Some are not healed because of their failure to receive the written promise of God as His direct Word to them. They fail to recognize that faith interprets the Word of God as the voice of God. In Psalm 138:2 we read, "Thou hast magnified thy word above all thy name."

21. Waiting for Healing to Believe

Some will not believe that their prayer for healing has been heard until they have experienced and seen the answer. Christ has not promised that our healing shall begin before we believe that He has heard our prayer. Some suppose that they must keep on praying, and not believe that their prayer has been heard, until they are well. This is exactly the opposite of what God requires.

In Mark 11:24 Jesus tells us exactly the conditions He requires for our appropriation of the blessings He has promised. He says, "What things soever ye desire, *when ye pray*, believe that ye receive them, and ye shall have them." That is, "ye shall have them" *after* you believe He has heard your prayer. As Jesus said, "I thank thee that thou *hast* heard me," while Lazarus was still dead; so we should be able to say, "I thank Thee that Thou *hast* heard me," while we are still sick.

199

"Ye shall have them," is your answer from Jesus. It is also your proof that your prayer has been heard.

As we have already remarked, faith interprets the Word of God as the voice of God. God has not promised that our healing shall begin before we believe that He has heard our prayer. "If we ask anything according to his will, he heareth us." If this is true, then we must believe that our prayer has been heard when we pray. We must be able to say, "We know we have the petitions that we desired of Him," not because we see the answer, but because "God is faithful, who also will do it."

Abraham did not keep on praying for the birth of Isaac until the child was born. Instead, he kept on believing and glorifying God for His Word in the matter.

More than once we have read that it was *after* Solomon had "made an end of praying" that the blessing came.

Jesus, at the grave of Lazarus, had "made an end of praying." Before Lazarus came out from his tomb, Jesus said, "I thank thee that thou hast heard me."

Jehoshaphat and the children of Israel had "made an end of praying." They were all praising God "with a loud voice" for the answer to their prayers before they went out to do battle with the three great armies. Their faith was "the evidence [or assurance] of things not [yet] seen" (Hebrews 11:1).

The 120 had "made an end of praying." They were all "continually praising and blessing God" when the Spirit was poured out upon them.

It is supposed to be the "end of praying" when one has been anointed for healing. If one who has been anointed really has faith, we will hear nothing from him but thanksgiving until he has been healed.

When a child begs her mother for a new dress, and the mother says, "I will get it for you," the child quits asking before there is any dress in sight. Instead of continuing to say, "Please give me a dress," she says, "Goody! Goody!"

Perhaps I should say here that after commitment, one must not become indifferent. One's trust must remain active. It must be like that of the children of Israel when they marched around the walls of Jericho and blew their rams' horns. It must be like that of Jehoshaphat and his men. After they had "made an end of praying," they went out to battle, singing praises to God.

The healing of the ten lepers came while their trust was still active.

God said to the dying Israelites, "Every one that *looketh* shall live." This word *looketh* is in the continuous present tense. It is not a mere glance, but a continuous "stare."

Moses "endured as *seeing* [continuously seeing] him who is invisible."

It was a "*steadfast*" faith that brought the fulfillment of God's promise to Abraham. Abraham became strong in faith by *looking* (continuously) unto the promise of God.

If we allow our trust to become inactive, it will weaken; if we keep it active, it will continually grow stronger.

22. Focus on Improvement, Not on God's Promises

Some hinder God by basing their faith on their improvement after prayer rather than on His promise. They do not realize that there is no other reason for faith as good as the Word of God. They do not understand that God wants to train every Christian to believe Him when everything they can see, except His promise, is to the contrary. Amen, and amen!

14

Paul's Thorn

And lest [i.e., for fear that] I should be exalted above measure
through the abundance of the revelations, there was given
to me a thorn in the flesh, the messenger of Satan to buffet
me, lest I should be exalted above measure. For this thing
I besought the Lord thrice, that it might depart from me.
And he said unto me, My grace is sufficient for thee: for my
strength is made perfect in weakness. Most gladly therefore
will I rather glory in my infirmities, that the power of Christ
may rest upon me. Therefore I take pleasure in infirmities,
in reproaches, in necessities, in persecutions, in distresses
for Christ's sake: for when I am weak, then am I strong.

2 Corinthians 12:7–10

One of the most prevalent objections raised today against
the ministry of healing is Paul's "thorn in the flesh." One
traditional idea has led to another. There is a widespread
teaching that God is the author of disease, and that He has
chosen some of the most devout of His children to remain
sick and glorify Him by exhibiting fortitude and patience.
This has, no doubt, led to the idea that Paul had a sickness
that God refused to heal. We do not believe that anyone

who would take time to read all that God has to say on the subject of healing could ever form such a conclusion.

I am quick to admit that equally devout men may hold contrary views, not only on this point, but on the whole subject of divine healing. It is merely a matter of study and investigation. Many good men, whose teaching has been that the age of miracles is past, etc., while reading the Scriptures have thoughtlessly passed over the Bible teaching on healing, believing it not applicable for our day. Nearly all who have spoken and written against us have not hesitated to use our name and "go after us with hammer and tongs"; but they never have attempted to answer the scriptural arguments that we have presented in our sermons on the subject. We have carefully, without mentioning their names, read their statements publicly and answered them from the Scriptures. If we were fighting against "flesh and blood," we would name them and go after them with a vengeance, but this would not be Christlike. We feel disposed to keep our hands off God's servants, and let Him fight our battles for us.

A Clergyman's Absurd Exposition

Before considering the subject of Paul's "thorn," we quote the following from a stenographic report of a sermon preached by a prominent New York clergyman. He also revised this sermon, printed it in great quantities and distributed it in every home in the vicinity of our revival. Although he had practically no knowledge of what we taught, having never seen or heard us, he sought to offset our teaching on healing.

Among other things he said:

> The fact is, Paul was sick. He was the sickest of men. He had one of the worst and most painful of oriental diseases.

He had ophthalmia, a disease of the eyes. The proof that he had it is overwhelming. He tells us that he had a "thorn in the flesh." When Paul stood before Christians, his eyes filled with unspeakable pus, unspeakable-looking matter running down over his face. Why would they have gouged out their eyes for him except that his eyes, as he stood before them, were a pitiable and appealing sight to them, as the eyes of any one with ophthalmia are? The particular pain of this disease is that it is like a "stake" in the eyes. It is beyond dispute that Paul was a sick man. He says so himself. Paul did not get this disease by infection. How did he get it? Jesus Christ gave it to him. Paul did not want to be sick. He prayed the Lord to heal him from this sickness. He prayed not once, nor twice, but three times. He received no answer to his prayers. In spite of all his praying he got no healing. His thrice-offered prayer brought him no cure, not even the hint of healing. That is not all. The Lord said to Paul a very startling thing. He said, "My grace is sufficient for thee." He tells Paul it is better for him to be sick than to be well. He tells Paul it is the Divine will he shall not be cured. He tells Paul Divine power can and will operate in and through him better with ophthalmia and sickness than without it. Hear what Paul has to say in response to the Lord concerning his infirmity and the will of the Lord that he shall not be cured of it. These are his words, "Most gladly therefore will I rather glory in my infirmity that the Power of Christ may rest upon me." Here is Paul saying just this, "I will glory in my ophthalmia. My eyes may be full of repulsive discharges; I may be the object of pity; no matter, I will glory in it. I will rejoice in my sickness." In the quivering flesh and painful suffering of His apostle, the Lord has written His Divine protest against this unspeakable doctrine, this *brutal* transmutation of the cross of Christ into a center of physical healing.

In answering our brother's arguments on this point, we will state, first, that the expression "thorn in the flesh" is not once used in either the Old or New Testament except as an illustration. The figure of the thorn in the flesh is not in one single instance used in the Bible as a figure of sickness. Every time the expression is used in the entire Bible, it is specifically stated exactly what the "thorn in the flesh" was, as we shall see. For instance, in Numbers 33:55, Moses told the children of Israel, before they entered the land of Canaan, "If ye will not drive out the inhabitants of the land from before you; then it shall come to pass, that those which ye let remain of them shall be pricks in your eyes, and thorns in your sides, and shall vex you in the land wherein ye dwell."

Here the Scripture itself plainly tells us that the "pricks" in the *eyes,* and the "thorns" in the *sides* of the Israelites were the inhabitants of Canaan, and not eye trouble or sickness. These teachers contend that Paul's "thorn" *must* have been a bodily affliction, because Paul says that the "thorn" was "in the *flesh."* I answer that, in the case of these Israelites, the Scripture says, "pricks in your *eyes,"* and "thorns in your *sides,"* but this does not mean that God was to stick Canaanites in their eyes and sides, with their heels dangling outside. God was only illustrating, to show that, as a thorn sticking in the flesh is annoying, so the Canaanites would, if left remaining, be a constant annoyance to the children of Israel.

The Canaanites Were a Thorn to Israel

Again, eight years later, Joshua 23:13 says, concerning the heathen nations in Canaan, "they shall be . . . *scourges* in your *sides,* and *thorns* in your *eyes."* So we see again that the "scourges in their *sides,* and thorns in their *eyes"* were Canaanites, and not sore eyes or sore sides. It is here again, as in all other instances, plainly stated what the "thorn" was.

Among the last words of David we read, "the sons of Belial shall be all of them as thorns." Without an exception, in all these cases, the "thorns" are personalities. As in each of these instances it definitely states what the "thorn" was; so Paul definitely states what his "thorn" was. He says it was "the messenger [Greek *angelos*] of Satan"; or, as translated by others, "the angel of the devil," "Satan's angel," etc.

This Greek word *angelos* appears 188 times in the Bible and is translated "angel" 181 times, and "messenger" the other 7 times. In all the 188 times in the entire Bible, it is in every case a *person* and not a thing without a solitary exception. Hell was "prepared for the devil and his angels" (or messengers), and an "angel" or a "messenger" is always a *person* that one person sends to another, and never a disease.

Paul's Thorn Was an Angel of Satan

Paul not only tells us that his "thorn" was an angel of Satan, but he also tells us what the angel came to do: "to buffet me," or, as Rotherham translates it, "that he might be buffeting me." Now the word *buffet* means "blow after blow," as when the waves buffeted the boat, and as when they "buffeted" Christ! Accordingly, Weymouth translates: "Satan's angel, dealing *blow after blow*." Since buffeting means *repeated blows*, if Paul's buffeting was a disease, it would have to have been many diseases or the same disease many times repeated, to be called *buffeting*.

In speaking of this messenger, or angel, Rotherham's translation uses the pronoun *he*, and Weymouth's translation states, "As for this, three times I besought the Lord to rid me of *him*." Both of these translators use personal pronouns, viz., *he* and *him* when speaking of Paul's thorn. These two pronouns, as well as the word *angel*, or *messenger*, prove that Paul's "thorn" was, as he himself plainly shows, a satanic personality and not a disease. We could not use the personal pronouns *he* or *him* when speaking of ophthalmia, or any other disease, because there is no gender to ophthalmia. Suppose I should ask a man how his cancer was. What would you think if you heard him reply, "*He* is lots worse, and I am suffering terribly." Now since Paul distinctly states that his "thorn" was the angel of Satan sent to buffet him, a demon spirit sent from Satan to make trouble for him wherever he went, why should *we* say it was something else?

Paul's Sufferings

Soon after Paul's conversion, God said to Ananias, "I will show him how great things he must suffer for my name's sake," not by sickness, but by the persecutions, which Paul enumerates as his buffetings. Paul had persecuted the Christians from place to place, and now he was beginning to experience the same and greater persecutions. Specifying the buffetings instigated by Satan's angel, Paul goes on to say, "Therefore I take pleasure in infirmities, in reproaches, in necessities, in persecutions, in distresses for Christ's sake: for when I am weak, then am I strong." Paul first mentions "infirmities," for he realized, and every Christian should realize, his weakness and inability in his own strength to stand up against a satanic messenger; to pass triumphantly through "reproaches, necessities, persecutions, distresses," and all the other buffetings he elsewhere catalogues. This is why he besought the Lord three times to be rid of *him* (the messenger) who was buffeting him so severely and in so many ways. Christ responded to his thrice-repeated prayer, not by removing the satanic messenger, but by saying, "My grace [which is for the "inner" man] is sufficient for thee: for my strength is made perfect in weakness."

When Paul saw that the grace of God was sufficient to strengthen him to bear all these things, he exclaimed, "Therefore will I rather glory in my infirmities [weaknesses], that the power of Christ may rest upon me. . . . For when I am weak, then am I strong." How could it be true that Christ's strength was made perfect in Paul's weakness if he was left weak, or unless Paul was an actual partaker of Christ's strength, which would remove the weakness whether it was physical or spiritual? Without God's strength being imparted to him, is a man powerful when he is weak, either physically or spiritually? Paul saw that the grace of God given to him made his very buffetings, even his imprisonments, to work together for his good and to turn out for the "furtherance of the gospel." What servant of God has not learned, and probably more than once, that it is when he is most conscious of his own weakness that the power of Christ rests upon him the most? It is when he is consciously weakest in himself that he is the strongest because of depending, not on his own, but on divine strength.

Grace for the Spiritual, Not for Physical Infirmities

Paul is clear in teaching that it is the "*life* of Jesus," which is "made manifest in our mortal flesh." It is nowhere stated in the Scriptures that God gives *grace* to our *bodies*. The very word *grace* shows that it was the "inner man" that needed help. The grace of God is imparted only to the "inner man," which Paul says, in his case, was "renewed day by day." In other words, "grace" is for spiritual infirmities, and not for the physical.

While the terms in the Old Testament "pricks in your eyes and thorns in your sides," were used, the Canaanites were not an annoyance to the Israelites in the sense of inflicting any physical disease or infirmities on their bodies. As the annoying Canaanites were outside the bodies of the Israelites, so Satan's angel was outside of Paul's body; for surely the apostle had no demon inhabiting his body. God's grace and mercy have always been given to enable us to bear our persecutions and temptations, but not to bear our sins and sicknesses, which He bore for us. God has never promised to take away *external* buffetings, afflictions and temptations from Christians. He gives us grace to bear them. But throughout history He has ever been ready to take away the internal, or bodily, oppressions of the devil, as well as our sins.

God Was with Him

Jesus "went about doing good, and healing *all* that were oppressed of the devil, for God was with him." God's Word tells us, "Yea, and all that will live godly [lives] in Christ Jesus shall suffer *persecution*." He has never said, "They shall remain *sick*," according to unscriptural views held by many today. This view denies all scriptural precedent. No doubt Paul got the expression "thorn in the flesh" from reading the Old Testament Scriptures. Because the term illustrated their external and not their bodily annoyances, he used the same expression to illustrate his own buffetings.

If the infirmities (weaknesses) of which Paul here speaks *were* physical, and, according to the above-quoted writer Paul was "the sickest of men," and God would not remove the "thorn" by giving him strength, how could he labor "more abundantly than they all"? If "the sickest of men" can accomplish more work than a well man, then let us all pray for sickness in order that *we* also may do more work for God. After realizing that God's strength was "made perfect in [his] weakness," then Paul could take pleasure, not only in his infirmities, but also in the buffetings that he mentions: reproaches, necessities, persecutions, distresses, etc. Note here, among other things, that Paul mentions necessities, meaning his financial buffetings, which he also refers to in his first letter to the Corinthians written a year before. He says, "Even unto this present hour we both hunger, and thirst, and are naked, and are *buffeted*, and have no certain dwellingplace" (1 Corinthians 4:11), showing that Paul's idea of buffetings was not a permanent sickness.

Paul Enumerates His Buffetings

If Paul's "thorn" was ophthalmia, or sore eyes, which he does not mention, instead of these reproaches, which he does mention, why does he not say he takes pleasure in sore eyes instead of in the reproaches? Not only here, but elsewhere in his letter to the Corinthians, Paul enumerates in detail his buffetings instigated by Satan's angel. In addition to the reproaches, necessities, persecutions and distresses mentioned in our text, in the sixth chapter of this same letter, he mentions stripes, imprisonments, tumults, labors, watchings, fastings, dishonor, evil report and deceivers. He describes his position "as dying, and, behold, we live; as chastened [beaten], and not killed; as sorrowful, yet alway rejoicing; as poor, yet making many rich; as having nothing, and yet possessing all things." In the eleventh chapter he mentions, "stripes above measure, in prisons more frequent, in deaths oft. Of the Jews five times received I forty stripes save one. Thrice was I beaten with rods, once was I stoned, thrice I suffered shipwreck, a night and a day I have been in the deep; in journeyings often." He also speaks of "in perils of waters, in perils of robbers, in perils of mine own country-men, in perils by the heathen, in perils in the city, in perils in the wilderness, in perils in the sea, in perils among false brethren." He personally suffered "weariness and painfulness, in watchings often, in hunger and thirst: in fastings often, in cold and nakedness." "Reviled, . . . persecuted, . . . defamed, . . . made as the filth of the world, . . . the offscouring of all things unto this day" (1 Corinthians 4:12–13).

Questions Worth Considering

Who but Satan's angel could be responsible for all these sufferings? In enumerating them we see that Paul mentions almost everything that one could think of *except* sickness or ophthalmia. The one thing that he does not mention, and that is conspicuous for its absence, tradition seizes on and says this was his "thorn." Why do these opposers substitute "sore eyes" or "sickness," neither of which Paul mentions, for all of these buffetings, which he *does* mention?

Although it is believed by many good men, one writer remarks that this widespread perversion of the Scriptures dealing with Paul's "thorn in the flesh" is certainly inspired by Satan, because it gives him the privilege of carrying on his evil work of afflicting and tormenting the bodies of humanity.

Since healing is an essential element of the Gospel, how could Paul enjoy "the fullness of the blessing of the Gospel" as he did, and remain sick? Is not healing a part of the bless-ing of the Gospel? Even such conservative scholars as those constituting the Episcopalian Commission on Healing agree that "bodily healing is an essential element of the Gospel."

Suppose our brother is correct in stating that Paul was the "sickest of men," suffering with ophthalmia, is it not strange that when the Ephesians saw the pus running from Paul's eyes and found that God would not heal him, this sight gave them faith for "special miracles" to be wrought on their behalf? It is stated here, "God wrought special miracles by the hands of Paul: so that from his body were brought unto the sick handkerchiefs or aprons, and the diseases departed from them, and the evil spirits went out of them" (Acts 19:11–12). The Scriptures never speak of special miracles in connection with any but this "sickest" apostle. Today, if handkerchiefs were brought from one suffering with ophthalmia, rather than laying them on the sick for healing, we would burn them to keep from spreading the infection.

The Case of the Cripple at Lystra

Again, when the heathen cripple at Lystra heard Paul preach "the Gospel," and got a glimpse of Paul's eyes, with their "repulsive discharges" (?), the sight at once gave him faith to walk for the first time on earth. Paul "perceiving that he had faith to be healed, said with a loud voice, 'stand upright on thy feet,' and he leaped and walked." This heathen cripple had never witnessed a miracle nor ever heard the Gospel preached until he heard it from "the sickest of men" whom God wills "shall not be cured."

Again, is it not marvelous how Paul, with "unspeakable pus, unspeakable-looking matter running down over his face," "the sickest of men," suffering with the "worst and most painful of oriental diseases . . . a pitiable and appealing sight to them," and "Jesus Christ gave it to him," telling him, "It is the divine will he shall not be cured"? Is it not marvelous how Paul, in this condition, could "make the *Gentiles* obedient, by word and deed, *through mighty signs and wonders*, by the power of the Spirit of God . . . from Jerusalem, and round about unto Illyricum" (Romans 15:18–19)?

On the island of Melita, after seeing Paul's unsightly disease, which must remain because "divine power can and will operate in and through him better with ophthalmia and sickness than without it," first, the father of Publius and then the other sick people in the island came and were cured (Acts 28:8–9).

Do the Sick Glory in Sickness?

The brother above quoted says, "Paul is saying just this, 'I will glory in my ophthalmia; my eyes may be full of repulsive discharges; I may be the object of pity; no matter, I will glory in it. I will rejoice in my sickness!'" Since these men teach it is right for Paul to glory in his being "the sickest of men," why do they not also glory in *their* sickness instead of doing their best to be rid of it? If they glory in their "thorn," why have some of them gone to a surgeon to have it cut out?

Some teachers hold that Paul's "thorn" was a partial blindness caused by the brightness of the divine light that shone on him at his conversion. In the year 60, when he wrote this epistle, Paul tells us that it was "above fourteen years ago" that he received the abundance of the revelations, which occasioned the giving of the "thorn in the flesh." This would make it twelve years *after* his conversion that the "thorn" was given. This epistle was written 26 years *after* his conversion. It would be well nigh blasphemy to speak of a partial blindness caused by a personal glimpse of the glorified Christ as "the messenger of Satan."

Why Paul's "Thorn"?

Paul distinctly states that his buffeting by the messenger was given him lest (or for fear that) he should be "exalted above measure through *the abundance of the revelations*." Is it because of the abundance of their revelations that the sick everywhere today must be taught to regard their sickness as a "thorn," which must remain lest *they* be exalted?

Since Paul's "thorn" was no hindrance to *his* faith for the healing of the other sick people in the island of Melita, and elsewhere, why should it hinder *ours*? Why *should* it be taught today everywhere as a hindrance to what little faith for healing the sick may have received? The Bible says, "faith *cometh* by hearing," but these days faith *leaves* by hearing—hearing these foolish doctrines. The widespread error concerning Paul's "thorn in the flesh" severs the Gospel. It entirely removes the foundation on which faith for healing must rest. The sick one must receive, from the Spirit and *not from the Bible*, a special revelation that he is to be healed.

We have noticed from the writings of these teachers that they are quick to mention the slightest physical defect in those who teach healing and are seeing the sick healed. Yet, they argue that it was proper for Paul, who is the most outstanding New Testament teacher of healing, to have, as they contend, the "thorn" of bodily affliction. If we could duplicate Paul's wonderful ministry of healing while "unspeakable pus" was all the time running from *our* eyes, would not this be seized upon by these very teachers as a ground for ridicule?

Paul's Thorn Not a Hindrance to His Labor

The Scriptures show that Paul's "thorn" did not hinder him from laboring more abundantly than all others. Those who are taught that their sickness is a "thorn" that must remain are often incapacitated by *their* "thorn" from *any* labor. They are not even able to care for themselves. They increase other people's labors by having to be cared for. It was the apostle Paul who wrote that we may be "prepared unto every good work," "thoroughly furnished unto all good works," "zealous of good works . . . careful to maintain good works," and "perfect in every good work to do his will." How can the multitude of Christians confined to their sickrooms by a "thorn in the flesh," "abound unto every good work"? Do these several Scriptures belong only to healthy Christians?

If Christ's words, "My grace is sufficient," mean that He is telling Paul to remain sick, it would be the first and only instance in the Bible in which God ever told anyone to keep his disease. The very fact of it being a solitary exception would prove the rule, and what the Scriptures abundantly show: that He healed all others. Why do so many of these teachers today reverse the Scriptures, and make Paul's "thorn" the prominent point when discussing healing? Why do they keep in the background the universal policy of healing revealed throughout the history recorded in the Bible? Paul's "thorn" did not hinder him from finishing his course for God (2 Timothy 4:7). Present-day teaching concerning Paul's "thorn" has sent multitudes, often after many years of terrible suffering, to premature graves, with their course only half run. This is a constantly recurring and horrible tragedy! Today many who are afflicted believe this latter-day teaching.

Many erroneously seem to feel that they should follow Paul by praying until God speaks to them; that as with Paul He wants them to keep their affliction. If God should give them a scriptural reason for their sickness, we would quickly say, "Amen!" for we love the will of God.

In Galatians 4:13 Paul says, "Ye know how through infirmity of the flesh I preached the gospel unto you *at the first*." Probably the infirmity here was physical, but "at the first" does not mean that he remained weak. Does it not mean that he became well? Why would he say "at the first"? Probably, as some scholars believe, this was just after his stoning at Lystra.

After Paul, in the plainest words, tells what his "thorn" was, how strange that ministers today should say it is something else. Why should they use it against the scriptural doctrine of healing, when Paul, himself, was the greatest teacher on this subject among the apostles and other writers of the New Testament?

Paul's Preaching Stimulates Faith

It was the Gospel Paul preached in Ephesus that gave faith for the "special miracles" of healing we have mentioned. He said, concerning his own preaching there, "I have kept back nothing that was profitable unto you." If all preachers today would keep back nothing that was profitable, they would surely all be teaching healing.

In Romans 15:18–19, it was Paul who said he "fully preached the Gospel of Christ" (preached the full Gospel), and made the "Gentiles obedient, by word and deed." This was done "through mighty signs and wonders, by the power of the Spirit of God . . . from Jerusalem and round about unto Illyricum."

Twenty-five years after he had become an apostle, he wrote to the Corinthians, "For this cause many are weak and sickly among you" (1 Corinthians 11:30). If Paul's "thorn" was physical infirmity, or he was sick, they would probably write back to him asking, "For what cause are *you* weak and sickly?"

It was Paul who wrote, "Know ye not that your body is the temple of the Holy Ghost?" "the members of Christ"; "members of his body, of his flesh, and of his bones." He wrote we have the "firstfruits of the Spirit" (firstfruits of our spiritual and physical salvation), "that the life also of Jesus might be made manifest in our mortal flesh" (2 Corinthians 4:11); that "the Spirit . . . shall also quicken your *mortal* [not dead] bodies" (Romans 8:11). Paul said Jesus is the Savior of the body, "the body is . . . for the Lord; and the Lord for the body."

Called to Be Saints

Paul is the apostle who wrote "unto the church of God which is at Corinth . . . called to be saints, with all that in *every place* call upon the name of Jesus Christ our Lord." "God hath set some in the church . . . miracles . . . gifts of healing," etc. He said that these "gifts and callings of God are without repentance" [i.e., are not revoked], and that all are commanded to "covet earnestly the best gifts."

Paul did not believe, as men are teaching today, that these blessings were confined to Israel. He did believe that the "middle wall of partition" was "broken down," that in Christ there is "neither Jew nor Greek," but that we are "all one in Christ Jesus." Accordingly, he heals the *Gentile* at Lystra crippled from birth, the same as Peter and John did the *Jewish* cripple at the Beautiful Gate. Paul also believed that the Old Testament types "were written for our admonition," that as many as are of faith are Abraham's seed, that "to Abraham and his seed were the promises made," and that "if ye be Christ's, then are ye Abraham's seed, and heirs according to the promise" (Galatians 3:29).

Paul on the Island of Melita

It was Paul who taught that it was "in Him" (Christ) that "all the promises of God . . . are yea . . . and amen, unto the glory of God by *us*." In other words, that all the promises of God, including all His promises to heal, owe their existence and power to the substitutionary work of Christ for us, that the redeeming work of Christ was for *all*. Accordingly, the very last chapter of Acts shows us that Paul believed and proved that it was God's will to heal, not some of them, but "all the other sick people in the island" of Melita (Acts 28:9 Weymouth).

Paul differentiated between miracles and healing. He did not believe in *every* person being instantly made whole, because he left Trophimus at Miletum sick. Epaphroditus was "sick nigh unto death" for the Gospel's sake (or from overwork), and from such he did not recover instantaneously. Paul was not a fanatic concerning the natural laws of health, which are as divine as God's miracles. He did not hesitate to recommend "the fruit of the vine" in the place of water alone for Timothy's stomach trouble.

Paul believed in the sick themselves having faith for healing. He did not say to the cripple "stand upright on thy feet," until he perceived that "he had faith to be healed." Jesus, Himself, could not do miracles in Nazareth because of community unbelief.

An Instructive Résumé

Is it not strange how any minister can set aside the whole Bible, as far as the subject of healing is concerned, keeping in the background:

- God's redemptive and covenant name, Jehovah-Rapha
- God's covenant of healing

218

- The teaching and promises of healing in the Old Testament types
- The universal precedent of healing set throughout the history of the Old Testament
- The words, teaching, commands, promises and healing ministry of Christ, by which He revealed the will of God for our bodies
- The gifts of healing set in the Church
- The Church ordinance of anointing, which is commanded
- The fact that Christ bore our sicknesses as well as our sins on Calvary
- The multiplied thousands of those healed since the days of the apostles, down to and including our days in particular

Is it not strange that they can set all of this aside, and, when speaking on the subject of healing, choose as their text the Scripture concerning Paul's "thorn," which scholars admit they cannot prove has any reference to either sickness or healing?

Thirty-one Questions

1. Since the seven compound names of Jehovah, one of which is Jehovah-Rapha (I am the Lord that healeth thee), reveal His redemptive relationship toward each person, do they not point to Calvary?
2. Since all the promises of God are yea and amen in Him (Christ), do not these seven names, including Jehovah-Rapha (the Lord our Healer), owe their existence and their power to the redeeming work of Christ on the cross?
3. Has not every believer the same redemptive right to call upon Christ as Jehovah-Rapha (the Healer of his body) as he has to call upon Him as Jehovah-Tsidkenu (the Healer of his soul)? Is not His name given for healing as well as it is for salvation?
4. If bodily healing is to be obtained independent of Calvary, as opposers teach, why was it that no blessing of the year of jubilee was to be announced by the sounding of the trumpet until the Day of Atonement?

5. If healing for the body was not a part of Christ's redeeming work, why were types of the Atonement given in connection with healing throughout the Old Testament?

6. If healing was not in the Atonement, why were the dying Israelites required to look at the brazen serpent, the type of the Atonement, for bodily healing? If both forgiveness and healing came by a look at the type, why not from the antitype?

7. Since their curse was removed by the lifting up of the type of Christ, was not our curse of disease also removed by the lifting up of Christ Himself? (Galatians 3:13).

8. Isaiah says, "Surely he hath borne our sicknesses, and carried our pains" (Isaiah 53:4—Note: see chapter 2, under "He Carried Our Pains"). Why are the same Hebrew verbs employed as are used in verses 11 and 12 for the substitutionary bearing of sin, unless they have the same substitutionary and atoning character?

9. If healing was not provided for all in redemption, how did the multitudes obtain from Christ what God did not provide?

10. If the body was not included in redemption, how can there be a resurrection? How can corruption put on incorruption or mortality put on immortality? Were not the physical as well as the spiritual "earnests" (foretastes) of our coming redemption enjoyed by God's people throughout history?

11. Why should not the "last Adam" take away all that the "first Adam" brought upon us?

12. Since the Church is the Body of Christ, does God want the Body of Christ sick? Is it not His will to heal any part of the Body of Christ? If not, why does He

command "any sick" in the body to be anointed for healing (James 5:14)?

13. Are human imperfections of any sort, be they physical or moral, God's will or are they man's mistakes?

14. Since "the body is for the Lord, a living sacrifice unto God," would He not rather have a well body than a wrecked one? If not, how can He make us "perfect in every good work to do His will" or have us "thoroughly furnished unto all good works"?

15. Bodily healing in the New Testament was called a mercy. It was mercy and compassion that moved Jesus to heal all who came to Him. Is not the promise of God still true: He is "plenteous in mercy unto all that call upon him"?

16. Does not the glorious Gospel dispensation offer as much mercy and compassion to its sufferers as did the darker dispensations? If not, why would God withdraw this mercy and this Old Testament privilege from a better dispensation with its "better covenant"?

17. If, as some teach, God has another method for our healing today, why would God adopt a less successful method for our better dispensation?

18. Since Christ came to do the Father's will, was not the universal healing of all the sick who came to Him a revelation of the will of God for our bodies?

19. Did not Jesus emphatically say that He would continue His same works in answer to our prayers while He is with the Father (John 14:12–13) and is not this promise alone a complete answer to all opposers?

20. Why would the Holy Spirit who healed all the sick before His dispensation began, do less after He entered into office on the Day of Pentecost? Or did the Miracle-Worker enter office to do away with miracles?

21. Is not the book of the Acts of the Holy Ghost a revelation of the way He wants to continue to act through the Church?

22. How can God justify us and at the same time require us to remain under the curse of the law, which Jesus redeemed us from by bearing it for us on the cross? (Galatians 3:13).

23. Since "The Son of God was manifested that he might destroy the works of the devil," has He now relinquished this purpose, which He retained even during the bloody sweat of Gethsemane and the tortures of Calvary? Or does He now want the works of the devil in our bodies to continue, which He formerly wanted to destroy? Does God want a cancer, "a plague," "a curse," "the works of the devil" in the members of Christ? "Know ye not that your bodies are the members of Christ?" (1 Corinthians 6:15).

24. Are the proofs of divine healing among the 184 persons who testified in this revival the last two Friday nights less bright and convincing than the proofs of spiritual redemption among professed Christians today? Are not these 184 who have been healed in better health physically than a like number of professed Christians are spiritually? Would not the physical health of these 184 compare favorably with the spiritual health of many ministers of our day?

25. Would not the argument commonly employed against divine healing, drawn from its failures, if employed against justification, regeneration and the doctrines of salvation be simply overwhelming?

26. Does the fact that Christ could do no miracle at Nazareth prove anything except the unbelief of the people? Would it be right to conclude, because of the failure of

Christ's disciples to cast out the epileptic spirit from the boy, that it was not God's will to deliver him? Christ proved by healing him that it is God's will to heal even those who fail to receive it.

27. Is not God as willing to show the mercy of healing to His worshipers as He is to show the mercy of forgiveness to His enemies? (Romans 8:32).

28. If Paul (as a New York minister says) "was the sickest of men suffering from ophthalmia of the eyes," or if, as others teach, his "thorn in the flesh" was *physical* weakness instead of what Paul himself says it was, "Satan's angel" inflicting the many buffetings that Paul enumerates, how could he labor more abundantly than all the other apostles? Or since he had strength to do more work than all the others, how could his "weaknesses" be *physical?* Since Paul's "thorn" did not hinder his faith for the universal healing of "all the rest of the sick folk on the Island" of Melita (Moffatt's translation), why should it hinder *ours?* Would not *Paul's* failure to be healed, if he was sick, hinder the universal faith of these heathen for their healing? Why do traditional teachers substitute "ophthalmia of the eyes" or sickness (neither of which Paul mentions), for the "reproaches, ... necessities, ... persecutions," "distresses" and all the other buffetings at the hands of "Satan's angel," which he *does* mention? If sickness constitutes his "thorn," why does he not say he takes pleasure in the sickness instead of the buffetings? How could Paul, sick in body, or with the unsightly disease of "ophthalmia of the eyes," and unable to be healed, "make the Gentiles obedient, by word and deed, *through mighty signs and wonders . . .*" (Romans 15:18–19)?

224

29. If sickness is the will of God, then would not every physician be a lawbreaker, every trained nurse be defying the Almighty, every hospital a house of rebellion instead of a house of mercy? Instead of supporting hospitals, should we not then do our utmost to close them?

30. Since Jesus in the gospels never commissioned anybody to preach the Gospel without commanding that person to heal the sick, how can we obey this command if there is no Gospel (good news) of healing to proclaim to the sick as a basis for their faith? Since faith is expecting God to keep His promise, how can there be faith for healing if God has not promised it? And since the Bible is full of promises of healing, are they not all Gospel (good news) to the sick? Since "faith cometh by hearing . . . the word," how can the sick have faith for healing if there is nothing for them to hear?

31. "Could the loving heart of the Son of God, Who had compassion upon the sick, and healed all who had need of healing, cease to regard the sufferings of His own when He had become exalted at the right hand of the Father?"

✍

Propounded by Evangelist F. F. Bosworth in the Alliance Tabernacle, Toronto, Canada, April 20, 1923, as a part of his sermon answering the question of an opposer, "Is There a Gospel of Healing?"

Testimonies

The following testimonies took place over a few years in the early 1920s. The original language and expressions were old-fashioned and we seriously considered dropping them in this revision. However, as we read and reread them, we felt that the testimonies were too wonderful to cut out. We did revise some of the language to make it more readable. We removed dates and addresses because after nearly eighty years, they are irrelevant.

These testimonies are only a few of the 225,000 that were received up until 1948. Then my father went to Africa and other mission fields. Until Dad's home-going in 1958, an explosion of testimonies continued to arrive from untold thousands who were wonderfully saved and healed. Dad was always excited to "make known His deeds."

Bob Bosworth

Miraculous Healing of One Leads Many to Soul Salvation—Physical Blessings Also Follow

The five testimonies combined under this heading call attention to the spiritual and physical blessings that constantly follow the healing of a single individual. The result of the healing of Aeneas was that all Lydda and Saron turned to God. His healing was as important as the salvation of two cities. Through the healing of the lame man at the beautiful gate of the Temple, five thousand men were saved. Paul tells us of God's purpose "to make the Gentiles obedient in word and deed through mighty signs and wonders."

The persons healed constantly receive with the physical blessing an infilling of the Spirit. They also receive a compassion that sends them out to seek the salvation of others and to tell them that they can receive from a loving God the healing that they need for their own bodies.

Thrilling testimonies telling of a "chain of blessings" are continually being received.

Saved and healed of her affliction, Mrs. J. B. Long, Pittsburgh, Pennsylvania, sought to fulfill the promise she made to take the message of divine healing to some sick friends. Prompted by the Holy Spirit, she went to the altar with her own bodily affliction. Anointed by the Rev. E. D. Whiteside and Evangelist Fred Francis Bosworth, she arose to be a spiritual blessing to others. How faithfully she fulfilled her promise is shown by her determination to carry the Gospel with its messages of bodily healing to the sick in soul and body. Souls saved and bodies healed bring a blessed assurance of happiness to the benighted and forsaken.

Cracked Knees—Painful to Walk—Now Climb Steps

More than a year ago I was healed of total deafness in my right ear and also cracked knee-caps. The deafness was due to a nervous break-down which I had more than ten years ago and it left me deaf for more than five years. On my way to church one night in company with Miss Elizabeth Taylor, I fell and cracked my knees. They caused me great suffering for several years and kept growing worse all the time.

I could scarcely go up and down the steps, but now, praise God, I can run. I live on a hill top. To take the streetcar, it is necessary to go down a flight of 185 steps. I used to suffer agony, holding onto the rail and trying to get down, but bless His dear name, I can now run down! I never go down those steps without lifting my heart to God in true thankfulness for what He has done.

It was during the first Bosworth Campaign in Pittsburgh, Pennsylvania, that I was healed. I sat in the meeting looking at the wonderful sight of people being saved and healed. I had been saved 38 years before, when I was just a little girl. The thought came to me that night, how sweet it would be to be able to take the message of divine healing to some of my sick friends. Just then I wondered how I could carry the Gospel of healing to any one, unless I have a testimony of my own. That convinced me.

Without the least hesitation I went to the altar with my own bodily ills and was anointed. Brother F. F. Bosworth and Rev. E. D. Whiteside prayed with me and I was instantly healed. My healing was complete. During the year following my healing I have never had any return of the trouble. I was saved to serve. I was anxious to be healed that I might serve Him better. As I walked up Ohio Street that night to take the streetcar, I suddenly seemed to be in a new world.

I believe that at that time God gave me a fresh baptism of His Holy Spirit. This has been the most wonderful year of my life, for God has so sweetly used me in His service. Truly, there is joy in the service of the King. I have had many spiritual blessings follow my healing and Christ has been nearer and dearer to me than ever before.

I find the great secret of this joy comes from testifying to the power of God. The night I was healed I testified to a member of my church on the streetcar. I knew it would spread. The following week my pastor called me aside, told me what he had heard, and asked if it was true. I told him it was true. He could not see it my way at first, but when I gave him Scripture for it (Matthew 8:16–17) the Lord fully convinced him.

The following week we started revival services at our church. It was the best revival we ever knew. One evening each week, our pastor spoke on divine healing. The invitation went out to those seeking salvation or healing. The pastor anointed, while Brother I. E. Hoover and I laid hands on the sick. Many were healed while we prayed with them.

I felt I was just an empty vessel lying at the Master's feet, ready to be filled and used in His service. The next day after my healing, I asked the Lord to send me to someone who needed healing, that I might tell my story. The face of a friend of mine came before me, Mrs. Sadie Robinson. I went to call and found her in bed, having been ill for many weeks.

The next day Brother I. E. Hoover offered his car; we took her to the Christian Missionary Alliance Tabernacle, where she was anointed by Brother Bosworth and was healed. It resulted in the salvation of four in her family. God has been wonderfully using her, to His honor and glory. One of her neighbors, Mrs. Bigley, a great sufferer for thirty years, whose testimony follows, had heard of Mrs. Robinson's healing and sent for her and myself. We spent an afternoon with her studying the Bible together. She was very excited.

I went again in a few days with Mr. Fred Collins, who was healed at the Bosworth meeting, Mr. I. E. Hoover and Rev. Kreamer, the Baptist minister. We prayed with Mrs. Bigley, anointed her and she was healed.

This was on Saturday. The following Tuesday she was up and perfectly well. She had her shoes on, without a sign of her old trouble. She was beaming with happiness and she has had no return of any of her troubles which had been of thirty years' duration. Her son was also brought to Christ and healed at the Sheraden Tabernacle.

I find that the most important thing in the Christian life is perfect obedience to the will of God. It is very sweet to live in the inner circle. Although it may cut us off from those around us, yet it is sweet to know we have His approval.

Mrs. J. B. Long, Pittsburgh, Pennyslvania

Mrs. Taylor Confirms Mrs. Long's Testimony

I am well acquainted with Mrs. Long. We both belong to the same church and I was with her the night she fell and cracked her knee-caps. She was laid up for some time. They were healed and she has no more trouble with them.

Elizabeth Taylor, Pittsburgh, Pennsylvania

Carried by Three—Came Out Alone—Was Almost Dead—Now Healed

HEALING OF NERVOUS BREAK-DOWN RESULTS IN SALVATION OF HUSBAND AND THREE DAUGHTERS

In the early fall of last year, I was taken very ill with a nervous break-down of my body and mind as well as internal trouble. I was kept at home for two weeks under the care of one of our best doctors. One day I would seemingly be better, but the next day would be worse until some kind friends came and took me to their home in the country. There I was free from all city noise and I received the best treatment and all the love and kindness that one could receive. I was there six weeks, but had just the same results, being kept under a quieting tonic most of the time, nights as well as days.

After six weeks, I was brought back, if anything, worse than before. The next day after being brought home the blessed Lord sent one of His faithful servants to me, Mrs. Mary Long. She gave me her testimony and prayed for me. She was all love and kindness. One day she mended some of my son's greasy working clothes, and another day helped the children prepare the meal. I tell this to the glory of God to show what one will do when the Holy Ghost has the "right of way" with them.

On Monday, November 15, she and two other dear Christians came with a car and took me to the Tabernacle on Arch Street. There, Brother Bosworth prayed for me and anointed me and I was healed immediately—Bless God! Jesus did it in answer to prayer. It took three to help me into the Tabernacle, but I walked out without the aid of a human hand, leaning heavily on the arm of Jesus.

Oh, He was, and still is, so precious to me. The morning of the 15th, when I was taken to the Tabernacle, my husband and family truly believed I could not possibly live through the day. That evening I prepared the evening meal with very little help from the children. My healing has been the means of my husband and three daughters giving their hearts to Christ. They are standing firmly today on the solid rock, Christ Jesus, praise God.

The next morning, the 16th, I took a streetcar and went to the meeting without anyone assisting me. Jesus was with me and still is. The day after that, the 17th, I cleaned three rooms completely, singing and praising God all the time. Since that I have been attacked a few times, and each time the dear Lord has sent Sister Long to me and she has prayed for me, and bless God, each time I have been healed. I truly have much to praise God for.

I knew Sister Long before her healing. I know how she was afflicted. Since then, she has been delivered. I praise God for the way He is using her to His glory. May He add His blessing to my testimony.

Your sister in the Lord Jesus Christ,

Mrs. Sadie Robinson, Pittsburgh, Pennsylvania

Nervousness Cured—Suffered for Years

Crafton, Pennsylvania—Miss Hazel D. Benz. I have suffered from a nervous condition for five years. The doctors said it arose from a spinal condition. I had no control over the muscles in my head. My face and mouth were constantly twitching and distorted. My eyes were similarly affected. My head moved about. Specialist after specialist was consulted. None of them were able to help me. They could not determine what caused the trouble. Finally, I heard of the meeting at the Sheraden Tabernacle. I attended November 4th. When the invitation was given I went forward, was prayed for and was anointed. The twitching and contortions stopped immediately and have not returned.

231

In a letter written several months later, confirming her testimony, Miss Benz says: "Since I was healed of my serious nervous trouble four months ago, my mother, sister, brother-in-law and step-father have been saved. I have gained eighteen and one-half pounds in weight."

Varicose Veins—Blood Pressure—Limbs Swollen— Trouble Gone

In commemoration of the birth of our Lord and Savior, Jesus Christ, on this beautiful Christmas day, I know of no better tribute than the testimony of my dear mother and myself. I hope in giving it, that it may be used to bring peace and joy to some poor tired sinner or to help some poor sufferer to be healed, all "to the Glory of God."

My mother had been troubled with varicose veins for over thirty years, as well as high blood pressure and swelling of the limbs, which developed into a dropsical condition for nearly ten years. She was unable to walk for ten weeks. About five months ago, my mother heard of one of our neighbors, Mrs. Robinson, being healed by "faith in God." The case was so wonderful that we inquired and found out that a Mrs. J. B. Long had taken Mrs. Robinson to some church; so we found where Mrs. Long lived and asked her to come and see Mother. Mrs. Robinson and Mrs. Long came and prayed with Mother and explained the wonderful things in store for all who believed. Later, Mrs. Long and three from the church came to see us, prayed with Mother and anointed her. Three days later, she could put her shoes on and walk, which she had not done for ten long weeks.

Meanwhile, Mother had read her Bible, and as God revealed Himself to her in prayer, she was greatly blessed and all the pain left her limbs, the varicose veins started to dry up and all swelling receded. Her general health became better and the high blood pressure began to disappear, something that the doctors had claimed was impossible except by electric treatments. They had advised hospitalization months ago.

Today finds Mother in better health than she has been in years and there has been no return of any of her old ailments. Glory to God for His blessings! Being saved and healed herself, she has found consolation and happiness in the work of God and in His promises.

Meanwhile, Mrs. Long continued to call on us. She was never in a hurry to go and always had prayer before leaving.

When I saw the wonderful works of God in my mother, I too started to search the Scriptures and found God's promises were the same to me if I believed. On one of Mrs. Long's visits, she told me of her own life and of others. After telling me it was the last day of the Tabernacle services, she persuaded me to go. I went with Mrs. Robinson and her husband, who had also been saved and healed. It was a day I will never forget as long as I live.

All the time I had been listening to the evangelist, I had been silently praying for God to lead me. At the end of his sermon, he called for all who wished to be saved or healed or prayed for to come forward. I went forward with Brother Robinson, and was saved by the blood of Christ.

I had been suffering from nervous disorders and bad health for fifteen years, and had been through three very serious operations. I never had a well day. After being prayed for and anointed by one of the workers, I came home. Glory to God, "by His stripes" I was healed! I have enjoyed my meals ever since, have never been bothered with any stomach trouble at all, and my nerves have been strengthened wonderfully. Mother and I are so happy and the further on we go the sweeter this life gets. It seems we both are getting the good things God has in store for all who believe. I also want to mention this: in one week I prayed to God for five things which a person would think were nearly impossible, but glory be to His holy name, I got all I asked for.

Please print this so that someone may see it, profit by our experience and get peace and happiness like we did. All who believe on the Lord Jesus Christ shall be saved. This is His promise and praise His blessed name, He never breaks His promises. Our Bible is a great source of happiness now. My one hope is that God may use me in the advancement of His work in any way He chooses.

We are thankful to God and will always be His co-workers here until He takes us to be with Him.

Carson A. Bigley, Pittsburgh, Pennsylvania

Vision Restored—Friends Overwhelmed by Simple Faith

I had been a church member for five years. I knew that Jesus was the Son of God and that He shed His blood on the cross. But I did not know, and had never heard that it was for me, that I was lost and that I could be saved and know it. I didn't have to wait until I died to learn whether I got to heaven or not.

However, I was proud of the church and would never think of going into another denomination's meeting. But I was in need of healing. I had been very far-sighted all my life and had been cross-eyed in one eye for fifteen years. I wore powerful glasses for over eleven years and had to have them changed by a specialist about every six months. When deprived of my glasses for just a few moments, I would suffer severe headaches, and could not see well enough to distinguish faces or furniture. Everything would be hazy and blurred.

A friend in Pittsburgh sent me a newspaper, *The Tribune*, giving testimonies and announcing the Bosworth meetings in Detroit. I went to the meeting January 11th, and was saved right in my seat. I don't remember the text or anything about that night except that I felt much lighter when I went out than when I came in. That week the Lord began dealing with me, and "behold old things passed away and all things became as new."

The next morning, I went forward for healing. Brother B. B. Bosworth prayed for me and I was instantly healed. He held up a card and I could read everything on it. I was dumbfounded. For two hours my eyes were perfectly straight and my vision normal. Then both went back and were worse than they had ever been all the rest of that day and all the next day. Some of the folks at home tried to urge me to put my glasses back on—they said that I would go blind. But, thank God, I refused and trusted Him. The following day my eyes were perfectly straight and kept getting stronger. Now they are just as normal as anyone's. I forgot to mention that during the time the Lord was testing me, I could read my Bible, but nothing else. Two weeks after the Lord so wonderfully healed me, He baptized and filled me with the Holy Ghost and still keeps me filled.

I do praise God that He put healing in the Gospel and that the Bosworth Brothers came to Detroit and told us about it. Since the Lord healed me, I have never had a headache from my eyes.

There is no one more real to me than my Lord and He is nearer and dearer each day. I could never begin to tell what He has done for me. Almost every time I give my testimony, I hear of some one who has been helped either physically or spiritually.

I praise God that He cares for all things that concern us. When the Lord told us to go to St. Paul, we had only two cents (Mrs. Monroe and I). After we told the Lord we would go, He gave us the fare. I had never heard of any such thing as trusting the Lord for financial aid, until Mr. Bosworth told of his experiences. "Faith comes by hearing, and hearing by the Word of God."

One morning, we had thirteen cents; after getting a light breakfast, we had one cent left. So we cried out, shouting "Glory!" into our purses. (No one knew that we had gone on faith.) At the exact time that we did this, a special delivery letter was sent to us with two dollars in it. Three days later, when our rent was due, the Lord sent in fourteen dollars. That is the way He provided. When I was coming home, we had five dollars and twelve cents. I asked the Lord for my fare. By twelve that night (Saturday), He sent it in and one dollar and eighty-five cents more.

I have had to rely on His promises for everything since, and He has never failed me.

Use this testimony as you see fit, by the guidance of the Holy Spirit, and all for the glory of God.

Mrs. Edith Watt Lau, Detroit, Michigan
(This testimony was given a year after her healing.)

Healed of Cancer

About four years ago, a cancer started on my face. It was at first, apparently, on a small wart on my nose. I kept scratching it until it became a sore, and then it was apparent that a cancer had developed. At that time I suffered very much. Before the second year the pain and agony were extreme.

It was necessary to keep my face covered, both on account of its appearance and the necessity of keeping cloths saturated with ether and anesthetic to check the pain. I spent about $500 for anesthetics during the last year I was sick. This was the only means of easing the suffering. When I removed the cloth, the pain was so intense that I was blinded and could not see my hand before my face.

I went from one physician to another in Ohio, Indiana, New York and New Jersey, wherever I heard of a good one, looking for relief. I am sure I consulted more than fifty of them. But all of them said there was no hope and that they could do nothing for me.

But praise the Lord, in September, I heard of the Bosworth meetings which were being held in my hometown, Lima, Ohio. I went, prompted by no other desire than to get healed. I had never heard the Gospel preached in this way before and went forward immediately. When I was asked to pray I did not know how, and the words had to be put in my mouth. As I repeated them, faith came into my heart, and I began to be very happy.

They laid hands on me for healing and as they did so, I could feel the power of God going through my body. It rose up into my face. The feeling was that of a tight rubber cap over my face which was being slipped off, little by little. When it reached the top of my head, I saw a bright light and I had a vision of Jesus standing right before me. Then I shouted in earnest, although I had not been able to do so before. As soon as hands were laid on me, the pain ceased and I knew I was healed. Others tell me I cried out, "I am saved and healed," and that I threw away the cloth which had covered my face. I was so happy that I was not aware of what I was doing. I shouted and shouted with joy, went home shouting,

shouting almost all night and continued shouting when I arose in the morning.

When I arose, my daughter had made breakfast. She looked at me and exclaimed, "Oh, Mother!" There was a mirror in the dining room and I looked at that. I saw that my upper lip, parts of which had been eaten away previously, was healed. It had been eaten away so that the roots of my teeth showed. During the night it had filled in with new flesh, was covered with fresh skin and was as solid and clear as it is at present. There were no traces left of the cancer except the scars. Two scabs which had been on my face were still there, but later disappeared. But wherever the skin had been gone, it was completely healed during the night, and the new skin had formed.

My right thumb had been crippled for four years. My instep had been broken. They were both healed at the same time as the cancer. I have not had pain from either of them since that time.

When I saw that my lip was restored, I shouted so loud that the home soon filled up with neighbors, to whom I told the story of what God had done for me.

My children took my healing as an indication that the Lord would soon take me to heaven and if I went out to the neighbors and stayed longer than I expected, they would come to see if I was still on the earth.

For two years I had not been able to eat anything except soup or milk. I could not open my mouth far enough to take in food, and had to sip liquid from a small spoon held to my lips. I was healed on Friday night, and on Saturday morning I took up knife and fork and began to eat just as I did before I was afflicted. When the Bosworth Brothers came to see me the same morning, I took a large tablespoon, opened my mouth wide and showed them how I could eat. When they came, I was out visiting the neighbors and showing them my face, but they waited at my home until I returned and rejoiced with me over the healing.

On Saturday, something had said to me, "Go into the water." Brother Bosworth explained to me what it meant and I obeyed and was baptized on Sunday.

As soon as the news of my healing spread, I had many callers asking for confirmation of it. I received letters from all over the world asking about it and one day I received nineteen. I also had many out-of-town callers on the same errand. I was able to refer them to any of my neighbors about my previous condition, as all knew it.

Three months ago, a doctor who had formerly prescribed for me came to my house. He asked me how I was getting along. I told him I was well and praising the Lord. He wanted to know what doctor I had. I told him, "Dr. Jesus." He said, "How long has he been here?" I answered, "As long as I have." He did not know that I meant the Lord Jesus Christ. When he understood he shouted with laughter and was very happy over it.

On Monday, after peeling apples, I went and prayed for a woman who had a cancer. She went to the meeting a night or two afterward and was healed. As I came out of her house praising the Lord, I passed the gas plant. The men working there asked me what the matter was. One of them must have been a Christian for when I told them, he began to shout.

Since my healing, a year ago, I have not had any symptoms whatever of the cancer or any pain in my hand or foot, but about a month before coming to Toledo, I let a very large lump of coal fall on my foot. I was very badly bruised. Three or four days before I came here, a piece of bone about one half inch long came out of it. After coming to Toledo, I was prayed for and the foot healed. There has been no pain in it since then.

Since I was saved, I have been called away many times to pray for the sick. In one case, it was a little boy, Billy Jones, who had been confined to his bed for several months. He was paralyzed and had bad sores on his back and face. I prayed for him and told the parents that in nine days he would walk. I said that, because it seemed that a voice came to me with a message. In just nine days from that time, he walked to my house, two blocks away.

One day last winter, I was without coal. I knew that the Lord had promised to take care of me, so I prayed about it. On going downstairs I found a lump of coal that filled a bushel basket when we broke it up. I never knew who sent it. When I pray for anything I need, I am sure to get it, just as if I had a friendly neighbor and she had given it to me. I do not always get it right away, but it comes nevertheless.

Just before I came to Toledo on this visit, I said to the Lord, "I would like to be in the Bosworth meetings once more." He immediately provided the money for me to go to Toledo. I knew I was going to a strange place so I said, "Lord, I know You are going to take care of me." Through no effort of mine, He provided a beautiful place for me to stay.

When I had the cancer, I was obliged to sell my clothes to provide money for the ether, drugs and other needs; so when I was healed, I was necessarily poor. He has provided ever since, and I have never wanted for a thing.

The first of April, we were exposed to smallpox. The authorities quarantined us and would not provide for us. I prayed and one day when we had run out of everything, there stood a man at the door with a great big basket of things. Both my daughter and I had a bad case of the disease, but had no physician except Jesus. We were healed without any scars.

After nearly three years of suffering, to be instantly set free is almost too good to be true!

Mrs. Alice Baker, Lima, Ohio

Miss Lida Clark's Confirmation of Mrs. Alice Baker's Cancer Testimony

I was present at the time Mrs. Baker was healed of her cancer. After she had been anointed and prayed for, she said to someone, "Take that cloth off." The other person loosened it from her face and Mrs. Baker took it and threw it away. She appeared to be filled with the Holy Spirit. She cried out, "I am saved and healed," as she sprang to her feet. It could not have appeared to the audience that she was healed, any more than it did to me. Her face was a horrible sight. It was a mass of blood, pus and open sores. But

239

she said afterwards that the pain had ceased and that she had the assurance in her heart that she was healed.

The odor from the cancer was so offensive that the worker who filled out her card was sick from it that evening and all the next day. But there was no odor the next night. I sat right alongside her and know that this was the case. And the cancer, the holes in her lip and all the sores had disappeared. She was healed—that was undeniable.

After her healing, I saw a physician who had treated her during her illness. After hearing that she had been healed, he asked me to tell him what I had actually seen. I told him that I saw her come in with the cloth on her face, was present when she was prayed for, heard her say, as she took the cloth off, that she was healed and saw her walk down the street without the cloth.

He said that it was impossible, that she could not walk out without the cloth over her face, because the pain would have been so intense as to blind her and she could not find her way out of the hall. He said, "Girl, you have been hypnotized. That could not be so."

I saw him again after he had seen her, and he said it certainly was a marvelous thing for her. He acknowledged that she had been healed.

Miss Lida Clark, Lima, Ohio

Monster Cancer Healed

Mrs. Jerolaman, Chicago, Illinois. I visited Mrs. Trina Odegard, Woodstock, Illinois, in May, and was greatly surprised to see her in the condition in which I found her, more dead than alive. We know she had suffered with ulcers of the stomach for 25 years or more, and were of the opinion she had a cancer. Her meal consisted of a half slice of bread, and when I urged her to eat more, she told me if she did, the pains would kill her. She was barely able to walk across the floor.

After I left, she consulted three physicians in Woodstock, had an X-ray taken and learned she had a serious case of cancer, far too advanced to even suggest an operation. The physicians gave as their opinion, she would never pull through. They gave her about two weeks to live. She decided to consult a specialist here in Chicago, and he told her the same thing. It was during this visit in July that she heard of the Bosworth tent meetings at Cicero and North Avenues. She was taken there at once and when prayed for, was healed instantly. She said the power of God went down through her body from head to foot during the prayer.

Her soreness, pain and suffering were all over instantly. The cancer was eliminated by the power of God. She was so hungry before leaving the tent, she could hardly wait until she got where she could get something to eat. She visited us the next day, ate the heartiest meal I had ever seen her eat in many a year and there was not the slightest evidence of serious after-effect.

It has been six months since her healing, and when I called her the other evening, she was getting along fine. She has gained weight and is hungry all the time. The people in Woodstock were astonished, as they never expected to see her return alive, after making the trip to Chicago.

It was through her wonderful healing that Mother and I were saved. We wanted to serve a God that was so loving, and we gave our hearts to Him right then and there. I am happier every day since I was converted.

These, however, are not all the blessings we received. I had been ailing and seeing doctors for almost four years. I was so nervous that at times I almost went into hysterics. I was terribly anemic, and also had internal trouble for which I had undergone an operation two and a half years before. After that, I was worse than ever, not being able to gain weight or strength, whatever I did. I took nerve tonic, blood tonics and serum injections. Nothing seemed to do me any good. I became disgusted with life and decided to stop seeing the doctor.

I thank God that He led me to the Bosworth tent meetings, as I know He wanted me to go there so that He might save and heal me. I was not saved before that, and my healing came as soon as I gave myself to Jesus. I am gaining weight, am stronger than I have ever been and am not nervous anymore. I also thank God for the perfect peace and joy that I have in my heart. Life with Christ is all joy and happiness.

Mother experienced a wonderful healing. One doctor said I had better see that she was taken care of immediately or I would not have her with me very long. He said that she must have an operation for gall and appendix trouble as the pains were so severe she could not sleep. She had undergone an operation seven years ago and had not been well since. She also suffered an abdominal rupture after returning home from the hospital and so dreaded the thought of another operation. After being prayed for, she felt the power of God going through her and cried for joy. Her pains have left her entirely, and, praise the Lord, the rupture is being healed.

Mrs. Killick's Testimony

I had suffered for years with a cancer on the leg. The pain caused me to tear my hair and was too intense to describe. The doctors operated but they brought no relief. For two years after the operation I had not been able to tie my shoe on account of the swelling. I could not walk properly, kneel down, do my work or go out. The cancer was melanotic sarcoma. I had been confined to my bed continuously for four months.

Soon after being anointed and prayed for, the pain instantaneously left, and the swelling rapidly disappeared. The cancer has now completely gone and only a few scars show where the black monster with its hideous head lived. The flesh has become pure and clean and my health is perfect.

After being healed, I went to the doctor, who simply laughed and said, "Well, I am pleased to see it, Mrs. Killick, but I will bet you ten dollars it will be back in six months."

It is now nearly two years and my condition is as described.

Mrs. Killick, Toronto, Canada

Healing of Miss Nix

In October, I was healed by the power of God from cancer, sugar diabetes and enlargement of the heart, a twisted spine, almost total paralysis from the hips to the feet, the condition of being a nervous wreck and almost totally blind. I had suffered from the cancer for one and a half years, and from the other troubles for seven years. I walked only with crutches and when I went out, it was in a wheelchair. The doctor who treated me said, a few weeks ago, that I had been one of the greatest sufferers he had known.

About the twelfth of October, I had a bad spell and sent for the doctor. He said that I had about ten days to live, and no more. On October the fifteenth, a little man, who was in the habit of bringing my newspaper, came to the door and inquired as to my condition. He asked to see me, but was told that I undoubtedly would not recognize him. Before he went out I knew him but was unable to speak.

He said, "Mrs. Killick, who had been healed of a terrible cancer, is coming here. Would you like to see her?" I nodded assent. She came to see me and told me that God wanted to heal me. She read the Bible to me and prayed, but I do not remember now what she said. She sang a hymn and I do remember that. It was:

> Were the whole realm of nature mine,
> That were a present far too small.
> Love, so amazing, so Divine,
> Demands my soul, my life, my all.

She departed saying that she would come back again that night. I lay in bed thinking, and when my friend who was taking care of me came in, I said, "If God has healed that woman He will heal me."

I asked the Lord what He would have me do, and I heard Him say plainly, "Put on your shoes and stockings." My friend said, "Dear, you cannot get up," but she brought the shoes and stockings. She lifted my foot to dress it and I felt no difference, but the moment the stocking touched my foot, I felt the power of God touch my body. It started at my feet, just where I was obeying the command, and spread all over my body. I got up on my feet, although I had not stood alone for four years. Then I asked to have my clothes brought to me and I dressed alone. I walked into the bedroom and did up my hair. My friend asked, "What are you going to do now?" I said that I was going to help her get supper. She asked me what I was going to eat, and I told her the same as she was. Previously, I had eaten only eggs and orange juice. I ate just what she ate.

I went to bed at nine and slept until six in the morning. I could not stay in bed, but got up, ate breakfast, washed the dishes and asked God what He would like to have me do to glorify Him. I heard Him say, "Wax the floor." The tempter said, "You cannot do that; you have not been on your knees for years." I waxed the floor from end to end, and Mrs. Killick saw it completed when she returned in the afternoon. She said, "I am going to give my testimony in the little Salvation Army Hall. Will you give yours?"

She offered to get a car to take me down, but I refused and walked all the way. When I reached there, the power of God so overcame me, I could not speak. I remained but a few moments.

From that hour to this God has given me strength and guided my steps. Last summer, I had charge of one of the largest summer homes of the Anglican Church. I often worked from six in the morning until two or three o'clock the next morning. I have been feeling perfectly well ever since my healing except for an attack of pneumonia from which the Lord delivered me without the aid of medicine or a physician. *My testimony has been a means of blessing to many. Some of the girls attending our own little Mission Hall, which I was led to open in faith, have been converted and healed through it.*

Do you wonder that I love God? He has blessed me spiritually as well as physically and I am sure I am the happiest woman on earth. *Better than my own healing, He has used me mightily to tell others what He has done for me. Many have been wonderfully healed.*

Miss R. Nix, Toronto, Canada

Miraculous Healing Followed by Conversion of Twenty Relatives

I have been suffering with stomach trouble for about thirty years. Twenty years ago I had the first operation for a tumor. I got to the place where nothing stayed in my stomach and I could not think of eating fruit. I have had three operations since the first one. I had fourteen different doctors attending me. I got to the place where I could not even take any more medicine on account of the condition of my stomach. I found I had a fallen stomach. Last June I found I had an inward goiter. My condition grew worse. At last I found I had cancer. I went to the Peoples Tabernacle at Bethlehem, Pennsylvania, and was anointed and prayed for. God compassionately touched my body, praise His name! I cried for joy. The Lord has never been so dear to me. I did not realize He loved me. Things are different. I see that He was just waiting to come and heal me. I am healed of all my diseases, praise His name!

What is still better, I brought my husband, mother, daughter, sons, sisters, brothers, sister-in-law, nieces and one nephew. Twenty in all, and they were all converted. God made a clean sweep. "Thou shalt be saved and thy house."

Mrs. Edward Bander, Easton, Pennsylvania

Healed of Bright's Disease and Other Ailments

While listening to the full Gospel, which I heard you preach in St. Petersburg, Florida, last January, I received untold spiritual and physical blessings. It was such a revelation to me to know that God is so willing to heal, that I hope and pray I may be used to tell others.

After seeing a doctor for five years for Bright's disease, high blood pressure (240 and over), sinus infection and several minor ailments, I was told that I could live only three months.

I had been to numerous doctors of high reputation in the United States and Canada (Mayo Bros. and Johns Hopkins). I went to chiropractors and osteopaths, and felt that everything had been done that human aid could do.

But, thank God, He wonderfully healed me physically, and I feel like a new person. I used to have spells three times a week, but they have not returned since. My blood pressure is down and the doctor told me that my heart was normal. I was able to immediately discard my glasses, which I have had to wear for years.

Lela Beach, Cornwall, Ontario, Canada

Nurse Healed of Varicose Veins

For the past four years I have suffered with varicose veins. It was impossible for me to stand on my feet, even for a few minutes, without constantly shifting my weight from one foot to the other. Three different times, for four months at a time, I was compelled to stay off my feet completely.

My limbs were so badly swollen and inflamed that I could not bear any covering over them. Even during winter, I always slept with the windows open and my limbs exposed to the cold air regardless of the temperature of the room.

Several days ago I came to the Tabernacle, and after receiving instruction and teaching on divine healing, I was anointed and prayed for. I am entirely free from pain in my body, and am able to work every day without any discomfort. The knots or lumps on my limbs were the size of hen's eggs, but they have completely disappeared; praise the Lord!

I wish to thank God also for the healing of my little ten-year-old daughter. She had suffered with chronic bronchitis all her life. She was continually under the doctor's care, and yet never free from coughing, day and night. Since being anointed and prayed for, she has been entirely delivered. We praise the Lord!

I shall be glad to have this testimony published for His glory and the blessing of others.

Beth P. Evans, Johnson City, New York

Lord Couldn't Wait! Eager to Bless His Children

Some time in December, I was unloading cars of coal. In some way, I twisted my back. I started for my home, but was picked up and carried home. I could not walk because of the intense suffering.

For three months I could not walk. For three years I could not sleep on a bed. I had to sleep on the floor, because I could not bear to lie on anything that was not perfectly flat. My left side was paralyzed, and I was so numb that I could hardly walk.

When I heard of the Bosworth Brothers coming here, and read of their great faith in the Lord for healing, I felt my time had come to be healed. I got a healing card. I came forward and found that I could not be prayed for until the card had been numbered. I felt like that man of whom we read in the Bible. Every time he came to the pool at the troubling of the waters, he was always too late. Someone else had slipped in ahead of him.

I was standing in front of the platform, feeling very disappointed. As I turned to go back to my seat, the Lord spoke to me and said: "If you are willing, I will make you whole!" I said, "Lord, I am willing." Praise the Lord, He straightened my back and healed my paralyzed side. I can go to bed now and sleep like a baby.

Praise the Lord, and may He heal all that come to Him is my prayer.

Harvey B. Whitecotton, Indianapolis, Indiana

Crippled and Deformed from Infantile Paralysis— Instantly Healed

I want you to tell everybody, and read this in your meetings, so everyone will know what God has done for me.

When I was one year old I had infantile paralysis. I had to walk on my toe. My heel was up to the top of my shoe. My foot also turned outward. Last Wednesday, February 17th, our kind neighbor, Mrs. Howell, called to me and asked me to go with her to the Bosworth meetings. She said that I would be healed. My Auntie, who is very old and who is keeping our home together for Father since my mother died with the "flu," said I should go. I came with Mrs. Howell for three evenings. On Friday, February 19th, I was anointed and prayed for. We had only reached our seat a few minutes when my heel went down and my foot went over to the other one. I felt just as if someone pulled it down and over to the other one. Now I can step on my whole foot and put my feet together like any of my other brothers. Today, three days after being healed, I'm learning to use roller skates. I'm the happiest boy in Easton. I am thirteen years old. I want you to tell other crippled boys what God has done for me. I will always thank Him, pray every day and ask Him to help other little boys.

John Jr. Snyder, Easton, Pennsylvania

Mute Woman Is Instantly Healed

More than three years ago through sickness, I completely lost my power of speech. I have had several physicians and all told me I could never regain my voice. Some of them told me that the vocal organs were paralyzed. During all this time I have never been able to make an audible sound.

I have also been a great sufferer from rheumatism and gall-stones. My friends tried to make me think it would do me no good to go to Bethlehem to be anointed for healing, but I came and was anointed and prayed for on February 2nd and was instantly healed. When I walked from the platform back to my seat I found my voice completely restored. After three years of total silence I could speak normally. Praise the Lord! My pastor, who did not believe I could be healed, was greatly surprised to find I could talk when I met him on the street. He said, "I have been a doubting Thomas, but now I am compelled to believe."

The pastor of the Baptist Church in Bangor asked me to come to his church on Sunday. After telling the audience about the miracle, he had me stand and show them how I could speak.

I was also healed of my rheumatism and gallstones. I am so thankful to God for His mercy.

Mrs. Thomas Hughes, Bangor, Pennsylvania

Woman Instantly Healed of Two Cancers—Answer to Prayer

Fifteen years ago my health broke. I was compelled to give up my work. My whole body seemed to be filled with some kind of poison that puzzled the doctors. For twelve years I suffered untold agony without any hope of ever being well again. Three and a half years ago I grew so much worse that I had a doctor for four months. I got worse all the time. I was later told I had a cancer at the mouth of the large bowel and it had fastened to the spleen. I grew worse and poison affected my left arm and side until I was drawn crooked. I would scream with agony and pain. I begged folks to hold my arm tight as it felt as though it were being pulled out of the socket. Later the cancer spread to my mouth, going in from the throat and under the tongue until it was as thick as another tongue. The roots spread out and wrapped around the membrane under my tongue. A Philadelphia physician, after treating me for a while, urged me to go to the Philadelphia Hospital to see if they would use radium. After several of the professors there examined me, they decided they could do nothing for me, as the cancer in my side was fastened to the spleen. The one in my mouth was attached to an artery. I came home to die. I was a hopeless case. They could do nothing. I started to pray to God to have mercy. I wept in my room alone. I talked with Almighty God, in Jesus' name, until He took all fear from me. I made up my mind to suffer until He called me home. I got to the place where I was taking eighteen doses of medicine a day. I took nine doses of asafoetida to hold my nerves and stomach and to keep me from vomiting. I had violent headaches and times of vomiting. I suffered this way for two years. I thank God for Christian friends who persuaded me to go to the Bosworth meetings being held in Philadelphia. I prayed about it until the Lord showed me to go. I thank God I obeyed. I heard the Gospel in mighty power preached there. I went to the enquiry room three times and heard the instructions. I then got the evangelist's book "Christ the Healer," studied the references and found that healing was for me. On Monday night, June 14, I went to the platform and was anointed for healing. Praise God! He met me right there and I was instantly healed. When I was being prayed for, I felt a shock go through my body just like electricity. It seemed as though someone grasped the cancer under my tongue and was drawing it out of my mouth. I was instantly healed then and there of my terrible cancers. I have taken no medicine since that time. I am eating whatever I want, and have no pain whatever. I thank God that the Bosworth Party came to Philadelphia. May God bless them, every one. I hope this will help some other sufferer find the glorious deliverance I have found.

Mrs. B. Edwards, Camden, New Jersey

Remarks by F. F. Bosworth

Possibly not one out of ten of those who have been healed have sent us their testimony. Yet thousands of testimonies have been received from those who have been healed since those published in this chapter. During the years thousands of our radio listeners, whom we have never seen, after reading our healing literature have written to us asking us to pray for their healing. We have presented these requests in prayer to God, one at a time. We are still receiving a continuous stream of wonderful testimonies from those healed of every affliction. Many have been healed through their own faith, which came to them while reading former editions of this book. As high as 72 deaf and dumb from birth, after reading this book, have been healed when prayed for during a single revival. Again we say, to God be all the glory.

Dear Reader, why not have an extra copy of this book to loan to your sick friends? You can thus save them from premature death to a life of service for God. What has been accomplished in this way is a wonderful story.

The Ultimate Triumph

by Bob Bosworth

T. B., "galloping" consumption—the prognosis was a death warrant. The future became bleak. In those days, there was no cure for this killer disease in its later stages.

Fred Bosworth was on his way to Fitzgerald, Georgia, to say good-bye to his parents. The doctors had warned that he would probably not live long enough to make the trip, but God had His hand on this young man. He arrived in a dying condition, but still alive.

Healed by God's Power

Bosworth met a Methodist woman, a "Bible woman," who used to walk the hills of Georgia and the Carolinas selling Bibles and preaching the Gospel. Mattie Perry looked intently at him and said, "Fred Bosworth, you are young. You are a Christian, and if you died today, you would go straight to heaven. But I am here to tell you that if you die today, it will be the most selfish act you have ever committed. God's plan is that we should live to be at least three score and ten (Ps. 90:10). What about all the people that God has ordained for you to reach?"

Young F. F. Bosworth said, "Miss Perry, would you pray for me?" She said, "I wouldn't waste my prayers on someone who is just going to lay there and die." Fred thought, *If I lie here, I am going to die. If I get up, I can't do any worse than that.* He told Miss Perry that if she would pray for him, he would get up. She prayed for him; he got up and was instantly healed.

A New Future

Fred Bosworth had no way of knowing the long, difficult and glorious road ahead of him. He did not know that God would call him to preach, make him successful and take him to other countries of the world. Little did he know that his own healing was a seed that would bear much fruit.

At the time of his healing, there was little biblical teaching on God's attitude toward sickness, but there was a lot of theological tradition that excluded healing in the Atonement. Praying for sickness with the faith-destroying words, "If it be Thy will," left the sick and suffering without a solid hope.

After God called him into ministry, during personal study throughout the Old and New Testaments, Bosworth received the revelation that healing was in the Atonement, and, therefore, part of the Gospel. When he discovered this truth, he vowed to God that he would never again base his faith and doctrine on human experience or man's teaching. He would base his faith only on what God said in His Word. He would pray for the sick only on that basis; if they dropped dead when he prayed for them, he would step over the dead body and pray for the next one.

The Sunset Years

Finally, after a rich and successful life and ministry, F. F. Bosworth began his sunset years. His compassion for those who were sick and suffering had driven him. Often he would pray for the sick all day and all night, never sparing himself. In weariness and deep fatigue he began to feel the effects of an overloaded ministry schedule through the years—it was as if he had already lived two lives. During World War II, with gas rationing, he was very restricted in his ability to travel to meetings. Yet it was difficult not to be preaching continually.

Restored—The Second Wind

There was a period of frustration. Was his ministry over? Had he run his course? He did not believe in the worldly doctrine of retirement. What was he to do? As he prayed and waited, God raised up a healing revival following the war. Many evangelists were raised up who needed the experience and wisdom of a mentor. He again began to teach the truths he knew, and found great satisfaction. This was just the beginning.

Breaking Free—Overseas Ministry

In 1952, at the age of 75, F. F. Bosworth went to South Africa as part of a team of three evangelists. He was part of the greatest ministry that ever hit that emerging nation. At the

Greyville Race Course in the city of Durban, the team had the greatest religious gatherings ever held in that country. The newspapers estimated that there were crowds of 75,000, with 25,000 turned away—there was not enough room to accommodate the crowds. Thousands of hungry seekers, from every religious, ethnic and language grouping, were saved and healed.

This was the first time that Fred Bosworth had ever experienced the spiritual hunger of what had been termed "the third world." For almost fifty years he had poured out his life in North America, a place that had become resistant to the Gospel. He asked the Lord to not allow him to continue ministering in America.

After the age of 75, F. F. Bosworth ministered for five consecutive years in intensive evangelism in different countries of the world. He again drew on God's "abundant" life as God renewed his vision and the strength of his youth.

The Ultimate Triumph

In 1958 Fred Bosworth returned from a year of meetings up and down the mountains of Japan. In January he turned 81. His family was surprised to see him retire to his bed. When asked what he was doing, he explained that God had shown him that he had "finished his course," his ministry was finished, and it was time to go Home. He said, "I sure don't want to hang around down here!" All the children came home, for the first time in sixteen years, and there was a great final reunion.

My father, F. F. Bosworth, had prayed, asking God to help him glorify God in his death as he had in his life—to die without sickness. About three weeks after he took to his bed, we were around the bed talking, laughing, singing. Suddenly

Dad looked up; he never saw us again. He saw what was invisible to us. He began to greet people and hug people—he was enraptured. Every once in a while he would break off and look around saying, "Oh, it is so beautiful."

He did this for several hours. Finally, with a smile on his face, he put his head back and slept. We took turns sitting with him. My wife, Stella, was sitting with him when she suddenly realized that he had stopped breathing. There had been no struggle, no pain, no sound, no death rattle. The psalmist had described it correctly—God had simply removed his breath and he was home! "O death, where is thy sting? O grave, where is thy victory?" This is the testimony and ultimate triumph of F. F. Bosworth and **CHRIST, THE HEALER.**

Listen to the Message That Has Inspired Millions!

Christ the Healer, the late F. F. Bosworth's pioneer classic on divine healing, is now available on audio CD. Let your faith be inspired as you listen to what the Bible has to say concerning bodily sickness and healing.

Boxed in a beautiful presentation folder, this ten-disc set makes a thoughtful gift for those who love to listen to books on tape or who spend a lot of time in the car, as well as those who are not able to read.

Don't miss an opportunity to bless and be blessed. Orders yours today.

Christ the Healer by F. F. Bosworth
Narrated by Robert V. Bosworth
Available on CD and cassette tape
$40.00 plus 10% shipping and handling

Orders can be placed through:

World Outreach Publications
P.O. Box 4402
Dallas, TX 75208

World_outreach@yahoo.com

www.christ-the-healer.com